Grammar
Clear and Simple

John R. Boyd • Mary Ann Boyd

Acknowledgments

Our thanks to

Erik Gundersen, for his insights and advice in the formation and execution of this project,

Tina Carver, for her support and confidence throughout the process,

Louis Carrillo, for his dedication to perfection, which was a constant inspiration to us in the writing of this series.

And our love and thanks to

Sarah and Aaron, Justin and Heather, Anna and Allison, for their unwavering love and support.

–J.B. and M.A.B.

Photo credits: Page 58, Abraham Lincoln, Corbis; Sun Yat-sen, Getty Images/Hulton Archive; William Shakespeare, Archivo Iconografico, S.A./Corbis; Jane Austen, Granger; Pablo Picasso, Getty Images/Hulton Archive; Leonardo da Vinci, Bettmann/Corbis; Ludwig van Beethoven, Getty Images/Hulton Archive; Giacomo Puccini, Getty Images/Hulton Archive; Albert Einstein, Corbis; Marie Curie, Bettmann/Corbis; Neil Armstrong, Bettmann/Corbis; Yuri Gagarin, Bettmann/Corbis.

Grammar Clear and Simple 2, 1st edition

This book is printed on recycled, acid-free paper containing 10% postconsumer waste.

2 3 4 5 6 7 8 9 10 QPD 08 07 06 05 04

ISBN 0-07-282072-1

Editorial director: *Tina B. Carver*
Senior managing editor: *Erik Gundersen*
Developmental editor: *Louis Carrillo*
Director of North American marketing: *Thomas P. Dare*
Cover and interior illustrations: *Eldon Doty*
Interior design: *Design 5 Creatives*
Production: *Betsy Feist, A Good Thing, Inc.*
Printer: *Quebecor World*

www.mhcontemporary.com

McGraw-Hill ESL/ELT

"Our beginning-level students have profoundly influenced our approach to teaching. We are continuously renewed by these students, who come to us with their unique needs and desire for security and success. *Grammar Clear and Simple* is for them."

–John and Mary Ann Boyd

For over 25 years John and Mary Ann Boyd taught in the Illinois State University Laboratory Schools while also teaching in summer programs at Harvard University and Saint Michael's College. They have taught in Fiji, Japan, and China and conducted teacher education workshops throughout the United States and in the Philippines and Thailand. The Boyds have written several English-as-a-second/foreign-language texts, specializing in materials for beginning learners. Both John and Mary Ann are past presidents of Illinois TESOL/BE. In 2003 Mary Ann was elected to a three-year term on the Board of Directors of International TESOL.

Grammar Clear and Simple is a two-book series for beginning English language students that engages them in meaningful language practice. Book 1 gradually and gently introduces beginning students to the basic elements of English. Book 2 builds on that foundation and brings students to a deeper and richer understanding of basic English grammar.

Each of the 12 chapters is organized into a carefully sequenced set of activities that guides students from **receptive awareness** to **meaningful production**. Every chapter presents a core a set of basic grammatical structures. Each structure (with its associated vocabulary) is the focus of one lesson. This format allows teachers to present, practice, and reinforce the target structure in a single class session.

The first activity in each chapter introduces controlled vocabulary through pictures. The second activity checks students' comprehension. It is followed by a spelling dictation of the new vocabulary. Subsequent activities integrate the new vocabulary into a **strong contextual framework**. This strong contextual framework promotes successful language acquisition through speaking, reading, and writing exercises and group work. Dialogs and narrative passages provide students with opportunities to hear and internalize the natural flow of English. The innovative and effective caret passages (the students must listen closely to the passage to find the points at which words are missing) focus students' attention on new structures in a gamelike format. Word searches improve students' retention of vocabulary and strengthen students' spelling skills.

Notes to the teacher and a tapescript of all listening activities appear in the "Back of the Book." A separate Answer Key for Books 1 and 2 contains exercise answers and midterm and final tests.

Through the activities of *Grammar Clear and Simple* students will learn basic English vocabulary, and will, at the same time, internalize the grammar underlying basic English. With this text the task of learning English is not difficult and complex; rather, it is **clear and simple.**

Contents

Overview

Key grammatical elements are highlighted with clear and simple explanations.

Icons signal that teacher's instructions and tapescript for the activity can be found in "Back of the Book."

Picture dictionary activities use warm, compelling illustrations.

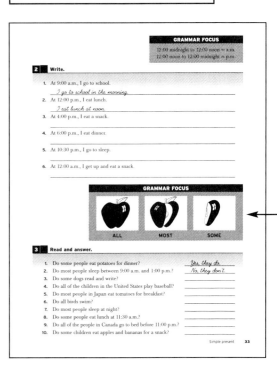

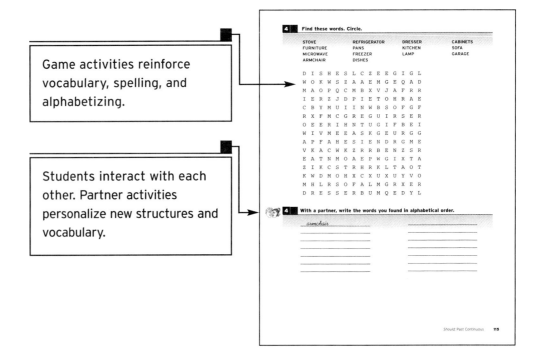

Game activities reinforce vocabulary, spelling, and alphabetizing.

Students interact with each other. Partner activities personalize new structures and vocabulary.

Vocabulary is introduced through pictures.

Matching activities check comprehension.

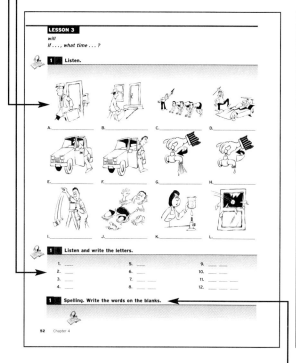

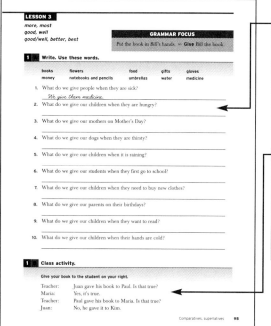

Strong contextual meaning is central to reading and writing activities.

Class activities create a context for meaningful practice.

Spelling activities reinforce new vocabulary.

Dialogs and narratives focus students' attention on the flow of English. Students first identify where words are missing, then write in words.

New in Book 2: True-false activities check reading comprehension.

To be, to have, to do

is, are

 1 **A** **Listen.**

red blue green white yellow	mother uncle aunt grandmother son	leg head chin hand ears
A. _____	B. _____	C. _____
tennis soccer hockey volleyball basketball	Sunday Monday Wednesday Thursday Saturday	Mexican Canadian Japanese Brazilian Spanish
D. _____	E. _____	F. _____
post office drugstore home mall school	A E I O U	B C D F G H J K L M N P Q R S T V W X Y Z
G. _____	H. _____	I. _____
cold/hot big/little old/young happy/sad fast/slow	gram teaspoon quart cup pound	dress shirt blouse shoes jacket
J. _____	K. _____	L. _____

1 B Listen and write the letters.

1. ____   5. ____ ____   9. ____ ____ ____

2. ____   6. ____ ____   10. ____ ____ ____

3. ____   7. ____ ____ ____   11. ____ ____ ____

4. ____ ____   8. ____ ____ ____   12. ____ ____ ____

1 C Spelling. Write the words on the blanks.

2 A Read and answer.

1. Tennis is a sport.   _True_

2. Green and blue are colors.   _____

3. Happy and hot are opposites.   _____

4. Wednesday and Thursday are days of the week.   _____

5. Your head and your arm are parts of your body.   _____

6. Brazilian, Canadian, and Mexican are nationalities.   _____

7. A, E, I, O, and U are all of the vowels.   _____

8. Gram and kilo are opposites.   _____

9. B, C, D, F, and T are some consonants.   _____

10. My aunts and my uncles are members of my family.   _____

11. Yellow is a sport.   _____

12. A mall is a place.   _____

2 B Listen and answer.

~~American~~	boxing	~~February~~	~~happy/sad~~	~~liter~~	over/under
April	brown	fingers	hardware store	~~mall~~	pants
arm	Canadian	football	hockey	March	pink
August	Chinese	gallon	January	May	post office
baseball	Colombian	gloves	jewelry store	~~mother~~	skirt
~~basketball~~	cousin	golf	July	nephew	summer/winter
belt	daughter	gray	kilo	nose	tablespoon
big/little	eyes	hair	Korean	orange	warm/cool
black	father	~~hand~~	library	ounce	~~yellow~~
~~blouse~~					

COLORS

yellow
_____
_____
_____
_____
_____

CLOTHES

blouse
_____
_____
_____
_____

FAMILY

mother
_____
_____
_____
_____

WORD

MONTHS

February
_____
_____
_____
_____
_____
_____

NATIONALITIES

American
_____
_____
_____
_____

PARTS OF
THE BODY

hand

OPPOSITES

happy/sad

PLACES

mall

GROUPS

QUANTITIES

liter

SPORTS

basketball

common nouns, proper nouns

GRAMMAR FOCUS		
Common nouns	**Proper nouns**	
hand, leg	New York, Tokyo	(cities)
soccer, basketball	Mexico, Colombia	(countries)
shirt, dress	Monday, Tuesday	(days of the week)
home, school	January, February	(months)
pound, liter	Anna, Martinez	(names)
green, white	Mexican, Canadian	(nationalities)

1 **Listen to the alphabet. Repeat it.**

A B C D E F G H I J K L M N O P Q R S T U V W X Y Z

a b c d e f g h i j k l m n o p q r s t u v w x y z

GRAMMAR REVIEW	
Singular	**Plural**
Yes, it is.	No, it isn't.
Yes, they are.	No, they aren't.

1 **Read and answer.**

1. Is *New York* a proper noun? _Yes, it is._
2. Are *January* and *February* common nouns? _No, they aren't._
3. Are *yellow* and *black* proper nouns? _____
4. Are *shirt* and *pants* common nouns? _____
5. Is *liter* a proper noun? _____
6. Is *Canada* a proper noun? _____
7. Are *volleyball* and *tennis* common nouns? _____
8. Is *arm* a common noun? _____
9. Are *Wednesday* and *Thursday* common nouns? _____
10. Is *Bill* a proper noun? _____

2 A **Rewrite the proper nouns with capital letters.**

1.	monday	*Monday*
2.	chin	*OK*
3.	february	
4.	tokyo	
5.	home	
6.	white	
7.	shirts	
8.	canada	
9.	june	
10.	head	
11.	united states	
12.	american	
13.	shoes	
14.	daughter	
15.	new york	
16.	los angeles	
17.	volleyball	
18.	sunday	
19.	gallon	
20.	rosa	

2 B **With a partner, practice spelling the cities and countries you have learned. Ask "How do you spell it?" Make sure the answer begins, "Capital . . ."**

Juan: How do you spell Canada?
Maria: Capital C-a-n-a-d-a.

3 Listen.

```
      ┌ Kim Lee
   A ┤  1428 E. Elm Street
      └ Los Angeles, CA 94231


                              Rosa A. Martinez
                               B   C     D
                              278 N. Jackson Ave., Apt. 305
                                       E                    F
                              Pecan, FL 33621
                                G   H   I
```

3 Listen and write the letters.

1. ____   4. ____ ____   7. ____ ____ ____
2. ____   5. ____ ____   8. ____ ____ ____
3. ____   6. ____ ____   9. ____ ____ ____

3 Spelling. Write the words on the blanks that follow.

A. _____   D. _____   G. _____
B. _____   E. _____   H. _____
C. _____   F. _____   I. _____

Martinez
Last Name

Rosa   *A*
First Name   **Middle Initial**

278 N. Jackson Avenue   *305*
Street Address   **Apt. Number**

Pecan   *FL*   *33621*
City   **State**   **Zip Code**

Rosa A. Martinez
Signature

Last Name

First Name   **Middle Initial**

Street Address   **Apt. Number**

City   **State**   **Zip Code**

Signature

1 A Read and answer.

> **GRAMMAR REVIEW**
>
> | Does he have a new car? | Yes, he has a new car. | = | Yes, he does. |
> | Do they have a new car? | Yes, they have a new car. | = | Yes, they do. |

1. Does your mother have green hair?   *No, she doesn't.*
2. Do you have two ears?   *Yes, I do.*
3. Does your father have blue teeth?   _____
4. Does your teacher have three noses?   _____
5. Do you have a neck and a head?   _____
6. Does a monkey have a right arm and a left arm?   _____
7. Do people have 20 fingers?   _____
8. Does a basketball player have four elbows?   _____
9. Do you have a wrist between your arm and your hand?   _____
10. Do some people have blue eyes?   _____

1 B Listen and answer.

> **GRAMMAR FOCUS**
>
> She has **some** nickels and **some** dimes, but she doesn't have **any** quarters.
>
>

~~bats~~   nephews

blouses   nickels

cats   ~~pencils~~

clubs   soap

gloves   tennis balls

neckties

1. She / pens

   She has some pens, but she doesn't have any pencils.

2. They / baseballs

   They have some baseballs, but they don't have any bats.

3. We / dimes

   _____

4. Sara and Rosa / skirts

   _____

5. He / water

   _____

6. Our aunts and uncles / nieces

   _____

7. My sister / golf balls

   _____

8. His cousins / dogs

   _____

9. I / rackets

   _____

10. My brother / shirts

    _____

11. Their sons / jackets

    _____

1. What's the opposite of *hot*?   *cold*
2. What's the opposite of *nose*?   *It doesn't have an opposite.*
3. What's the opposite of *fast*? _____
4. What's the opposite of *Tuesday*? _____
5. What's the opposite of *summer*? _____
6. What's the opposite of *library*? _____
7. What's the opposite of *long*? _____
8. What's the opposite of *new*? _____
9. What's the opposite of *rabbit*? _____
10. What's the opposite of *to the right*? _____

3 B   **Listen and answer.**

4 A   **Listen and put in 15 carets (˄).**

Allison:	Dad, what is the capital city ˄ California?
Dad:	I know. Ask your mother.
Allison:	Mom, what's capital of California?
Mom:	I don't know. Ask your grandmother. Know.
Allison:	Grandma, you know California's capital city?
Grandmother:	Sacramento.
Allison:	Is Sacramento words?
Grandmother:	No, it's just word.
Allison:	Are there two *e*'s Sacramento?
Grandmother:	No, just one *e*, but it two *a*'s.
Allison:	It capital S-a-c-r-a-m-e-n-t-o?
Grandmother:	Yes, that's right. It's Spanish word. There a lot cities in California that Spanish names.

4 **Write these words above the carets.**

a   are   do   don't   has   have   in   is   it's   of   of   one   she'll   the   two

5 **Find these words. Circle.**

COLORS	FAMILY	BODY	SPORTS
MONTHS	NATIONALITIES	PLACES	VOWELS
CONSONANTS	OPPOSITES	QUANTITIES	CLOTHES

```
O L T R C S S M Y E S M F X S
P G M S O C R D S E B C T E R
P V E S N N O O C J S A I C H
O H F J S B W A L I O T Z L G
S Y A V O X L H Q O I Q M O U
I I M L N P O D I L S U G T L
T Z I F A R S Y A R B A G H Q
E V L W N Z I N R E Z N Q E W
S G Y V T B O Y G J D T B S F
B K D K S I N Q Q Q X I R M M
I S Q K T M O N T H S T N M L
U L W A S P O R T S A I L O K
A T N S L E W O W Y P E P P Z
C P U G Z X T M Y K M S Y Y Q
C O L O R S O E V O W E L S M
```

5 **With a partner, write the words you found in alphabetical order.**

body _____

_____

_____

_____

_____

nationalities _____

_____

_____

_____

_____

prepositions of place

1 A   Listen.

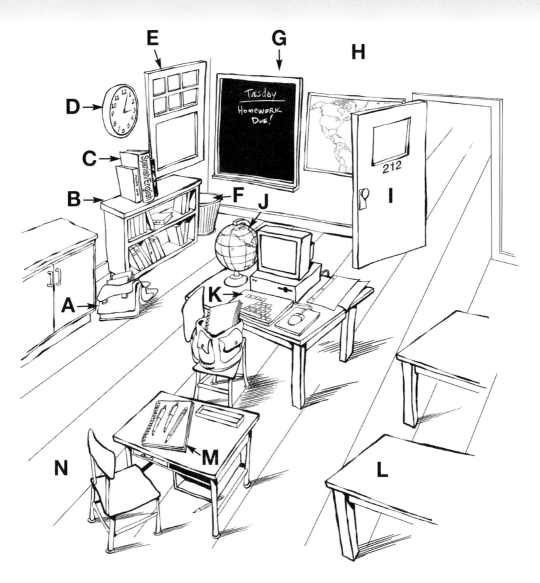

1 B   Listen and write the letters.

1. ____
2. ____
3. ____
4. ____ ____

5. ____ ____
6. ____ ____
7. ____ ____
8. ____ ____

9. ____ ____ ____
10. ____ ____ ____
11. ____ ____ ____
12. ____ ____ ____

Spelling. Write the words on the blanks below.

A. _____   H. _____

B. _____   I. _____

C. _____   J. _____

D. _____   K. _____

E. _____   L. _____

F. _____   M. _____

G. _____   N. _____

GRAMMAR FOCUS

to the right of
                    = next to   = beside
to the left of

2 Look at the picture, read, and answer.

1. The clock is on the door.   *False*

2. The map is behind the door.   _____

3. There's a notebook under the desk.   _____

4. The wastebasket is above the window.   _____

5. There's a book bag on the chair in front of the computer.   _____

6. The dictionary is between two books.   _____

7. The door is beside the window.   _____

8. There's a pencil on the floor under the desk.   _____

9. There are two sheets of paper next to the computer.   _____

10. The computer keyboard is in front of the computer.   _____

11. There's a number on the wall next to the board.   _____

12. There's a book bag beside the bookcase.   _____

2 Listen and answer.

Prepositions   **15**

3 B   Read and answer. Use these words in your answers.

a chair	on the wall above the computer
a notebook	the dictionary and a sheet of paper
next to the door	the keyboard
on the board	the room number
on the bookcase	the window
on the desk	under the table

1. Where's the globe? _On the bookcase._
2. What's in front of the computer? _The keyboard._
3. Where's the clock? _____
4. What's on the desk? _____
5. What's under the desk? _____
6. Where's the bookcase? _____
7. Where's the wastebasket? _____
8. What's in front of the table? _____
9. What's on the door? _____
10. Where's the dictionary? _____
11. What's behind the globe? _____
12. Where's the alphabet? _____

4 A   Class Activity. Tell where things are in your classroom. Make a list on the board.

The clock is on the wall next to the door.

The computer is on the teacher's desk.

4 B   With a partner, ask and answer questions about this.

Juan: Where is the clock?
Maria: On the wall.

Maria: What's on the teacher's desk?
Juan: The computer.

who?, what?, where?, how many?

1 A **Listen.**

A._____

B._____

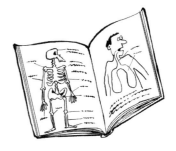

C._____

D._____

E._____

F._____

G._____

H._____

I._____

1 B Listen and write the letters.

1. ____

2. ____

3. ____

4. ____ ____

5. ____ ____

6. ____ ____

7. ____ ____

8. ____ ____

9. ____ ____

10. ____ ____ ____

1 C Spelling. Write the words on the blanks.

2 A Read and answer.

1. In what class do we study painting?   *art* _____

2. In what class do we study the body? _____

3. In what class do we study numbers? _____

4. In what class do we study sports? _____

5. In what class do we study countries? _____

6. In what class do we study keyboarding? _____

7. In what class do we study nouns and verbs? _____

8. In what class do we study insects? _____

9. In what class do we study people and dates? _____

2 B Listen and answer.

2 C Optional activity. With a partner, write sentences.

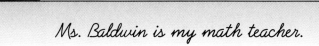

Ms. Baldwin is my math teacher.

Mr. Palmer is our English teacher.

Student Name:		Keiko Yamaguchi				
CLASS / ROOM	**M**	**T**	**W**	**Th**	**F**	
History / 310	9:00 10:15		9:00 10:15		9:00 10:15	
Math / 202	11:00 11:55		11:00 11:55		11:00 11:55	
Art / 105				2:00 3:30		
English / 212	3:00 4:00	3:00 4:00	3:00 4:00		3:00 4:00	
Health / 314			5:00 6:55			
Computer Science / 340		5:00 6:15		5:00 6:15		

3 Look at the schedules and answer.

1. Who has math at 4:30?   *Miguel does.*
   Where?   *In room 151.*
   How many days a week?   *Two days a week.*
2. Who has art in room 105?   *Keiko and Miguel do.*
   When?   *At 2:00.*
   How many days a week?   *One day a week.*
3. Who has geography at 7:00?   _____
   Where?   _____
   How many days a week?   _____
4. Who has health in room 314?   _____
   When?   _____
   How many days a week?   _____

CLASS / ROOM	M	T	W	Th	F
Student Name: Miguel Santos					
History / 310	9:00 10:15		9:00 10:15		9:00 10:15
Biology / 223	1:00 2:30		1:00 2:30		1:00 2:30
Art / 105				2:00 3:30	
English / 212	3:00 4:00	3:00 4:00	3:00 4:00		3:00 4:00
Math / 151		4:30 5:30		4:30 5:30	
Geography / 235		7:00 7:55		7:00 7:55	

5. Who has English at 3:00? _____
   Where? _____
   How many days a week? _____
6. Who has biology in room 223? _____
   When? _____
   How many days a week? _____
7. Who has computer class at 5:00? _____
   Where? _____
   How many days a week? _____
8. Who has history in room 310? _____
   When? _____
   How many days a week? _____

Miguel has English at 3:00. Keiko has English at 3:00.	=	Miguel and Keiko have English **at the same time.**
Miguel has English in room 212. Keiko has English in room 212.	=	Miguel and Keiko have English **in the same room.**
Miguel has English with Mr. Martin. Keiko has English with Mr. Martin.	=	Miguel and Keiko have English **with the same teacher.**

4 **Optional Class Activity. Divide into groups and write sentences about your classes.**

Juan and I have history at the same time.

Juan and I have biology in the same room.

Juan and I have art with the same teacher.

5 **Listen and put in 16 carets ($_\wedge$).**

Marlena: Can you tell where the art room is?

Rita: Sure, what's number?

Marlena: Let's see. It's 105.

Rita: Oh, that's to the gym. Do you where that is?

Marlena: I don't know where any the rooms are.

Rita: What hour is art class?

Marlena: It's 10:00.

Rita: Hey, we have the class. Let's see, it's 8:55 now. What class you have at 9:00?

Marlena: History. It's room 210.

Rita: Great, we have the same history too. After history class, we go to art class together.

Marlena: When do you have lunch?

Rita: At 11:00.

Marlena: Me too. Can we lunch together? I don't know anybody.

Rita: Sure. I eat lunch Maria, Juan, and Sara. We can have lunch together.

all	at	can	class	do	eat	in	its
know	me	next	of	room	same	with	your

GRAMMAR FOCUS

Contractions

am, is, are

I am	I'm		what is	what's
you are	you're		where is	where's
he is	he's		who is	who's
she is	she's			
it is	it's		there is	there's
we are	we're			
you are	you're		that is	that's
they are	they're			

will

I will	I'll
you will	you'll
he will	he'll
she will	she'll
it will	it'll
we will	we'll
you will	you'll
they will	they'll

not

is not	isn't
are not	aren't
was not	wasn't
were not	weren't
does not	doesn't
do not	don't
did not	didn't
will not	won't
cannot	can't

the same as
this, that, these, those

1 **Look at the Roman numerals.**

I	1	V	5	IX	9	XIX	19
II	2	VI	6	X	10	XX	20
III	3	VII	7	XI	11	XXIV	24
IV	4	VIII	8	XII	12	XXIX	29

1 **Read and answer.**

1. Is III the same as 3?   *Yes*
2. Is VI the same as 4?   *No*
3. Is XI the same as 9? _____
4. Is XIV the same as 14? _____
5. Is XXXIX the same as 41? _____
6. Is V more than 5? _____
7. Is X more than 10? _____
8. Is XXVI more than 25? _____
9. Is XXIX more than 30? _____
10. Is XXXIV more than 34? _____
11. Is VIII less than 9? _____
12. Is XIV less than 11? _____
13. Is XIX less than 20? _____
14. Is XXV less than 24? _____
15. Is XXXVI less than 35? _____

A._____

B._____

C._____

D._____

E._____

F._____

G._____

H._____

I._____

2 B Listen and write the letters.

1. ____   4. ____ ____   7. ____ ____ ____

2. ____   5. ____ ____   8. ____ ____ ____

3. ____   6. ____ ____   9. ____ ____ ____

2 C Spelling. Write the words on the blanks.

3 A Listen.

A. This is a Roman numeral.

B. That is a Roman numeral.

C. These are Roman numerals.

D. Those are Roman numerals.

3 B Read and write.

Sam   Mark

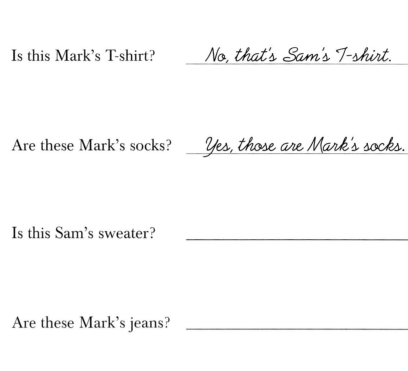

1. Is this Mark's T-shirt?   *No, that's Sam's T-shirt.*

2. Are these Mark's socks?   *Yes, those are Mark's socks.*

3. Is this Sam's sweater?   _____

4. Are these Mark's jeans?   _____

5. Is this Sam's hat?   _____

6. Are these Mark's boots?   _____

7. Are these Sam's shorts?   _____

4 Class Activity. Write your last name in big letters on a half sheet of paper. Give it to your teacher. Your teacher will hold up the names and ask questions.

Teacher: Juan, is *this* your last name?

Juan: No, *that's* Maria's last name.

Teacher: Juan, are *these* Maria's and Paul's last names?

Juan: Yes, *those* are Maria's and Paul's last names.

MATH	HISTORY	ENGLISH	GEOGRAPHY
HEALTH	BIOLOGY	ART	COMPUTER
CLASS	SCHEDULE	TEACHER	NUMERAL

```
Z  M  K  T  X  K  N  U  M  E  R  A  L  O  M
U  F  R  N  W  F  O  U  F  W  R  Q  Q  T  H
M  A  Q  E  V  I  X  T  G  U  R  H  G  E  O
R  A  T  V  P  N  O  V  S  T  I  I  C  A  K
G  W  T  R  H  H  E  S  S  R  G  S  J  C  D
E  E  R  H  Y  F  A  P  J  C  P  T  E  H  Y
N  A  O  L  U  L  Z  W  V  O  K  O  B  E  A
G  H  T  G  C  G  Y  V  W  M  S  R  I  R  O
L  K  M  F  R  S  S  J  N  P  A  Y  O  J  T
I  O  N  N  Q  A  F  D  W  U  E  D  L  Z  S
S  U  D  T  M  K  P  L  N  T  N  N  O  U  A
H  N  G  L  I  S  N  H  U  E  X  C  G  C  L
S  C  H  E  D  U  L  E  Y  R  S  R  Y  H  C
N  U  P  E  R  P  L  H  E  A  L  T  H  F  R
K  V  Y  X  S  Z  L  S  K  S  W  P  O  E  B
```

5 B   With a partner, write the words you found in alphabetical order.

_____   _____

_biology_____   _____

_____   _____

_____   _schedule_____

_____

③ Simple present

simple present

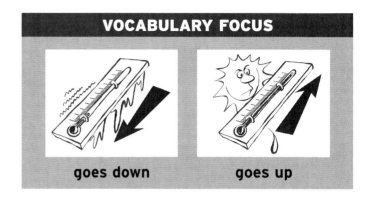

1 A Listen.

A. the _____

B. _____

C. the _____

D. _____

E. _____

F. _____

G. _____

H. _____

I. the _____

J. _____

1 B Listen and write the letters.

1. ___   4. ___ ___   7. ___ ___
2. ___   5. ___ ___   8. ___ ___ ___
3. ___   6. ___ ___   9. ___ ___ ___

1 C Spelling. Write the words on the blanks.

2 A Read and answer.

1. Does the sun set in the west?   _Yes_
2. Does the temperature usually fall in the summer?   _____
3. Do the moon and stars shine at night?   _____
4. Do the planets circle the sun?   _____
5. Does the sun shine at night?   _____
6. Does the sun rise in the east?   _____
7. Do flowers grow on the moon?   _____
8. Does snow fall in winter?   _____
9. Does your hair grow at night?   _____
10. Does the earth turn from east to west?   _____

2 B Listen and answer.

2 C Write sentences.

1. sun / in the west   _The sun sets in the west._
2. stars / at night   _The stars shine at night._
3. planets / the sun   _____
4. temperature / in winter   _____
5. sun / in the east   _____
6. moon / at night   _____
7. temperature / in summer   _____
8. moon / the earth   _____

A._____

B._____

C._____

D._____

E._____

F._____

G._____

H._____

I._____

J._____

K._____

L._____

3 B Listen and write the letters.

1. ____
2. ____
3. ____
4. ____ ____
5. ____ ____

6. ____ ____
7. ____ ____
8. ____ ____ ____
9. ____ ____ ____
10. ____ ____ ____

3 C Spelling. Write the words on the blanks.

4   Read and answer.

1. Do basketballs bounce?   _Yes, they do._
2. Does wood burn?   _Yes, it does._
3. Do chickens climb?   _____
4. Do rubber bands stretch?   _____
5. Does ice melt?   _____
6. Do butterflies run?   _____
7. Does water freeze?   _____
8. Do tomatoes bounce?   _____
9. Do cats climb?   _____
10. Does water burn?   _____

4   Listen and answer.

4   Write sentences.

1. balls / bounce / eggs

   Balls bounce but eggs don't.

2. wood / burn / paper

   Wood burns and paper does too.

3. ducks / swim / chickens

   _____

4. people / read / animals

   _____

5. ice / melts / wood

   _____

6. children / climb / cats

   _____

7. rubber bands / stretch / paper clips

   _____

8. water / freezes / milk

   _____

9. butterflies / fly / spiders

   _____

10. flowers / grow / trees

    _____

all, most, some
always, usually, sometimes, never
ever

1 A Listen.

A._____ B._____ C._____

D._____ E._____ F._____ G._____

H._____ I._____ J._____

1 B Listen and write the letters.

1. ____	4. ____ ____	7. ____ ____ ____
2. ____	5. ____ ____	8. ____ ____ ____
3. ____	6. ____ ____	9. ____ ____ ____

1 C Spelling. Write the words on the blanks.

GRAMMAR FOCUS

12:00 midnight to 12:00 noon = a.m.
12:00 noon to 12:00 midnight = p.m.

2 Write.

1. At 9:00 a.m., I go to school.

   I go to school in the morning.

2. At 12:00 p.m., I eat lunch.

   I eat lunch at noon.

3. At 4:00 p.m., I eat a snack.

   _____

4. At 6:00 p.m., I eat dinner.

   _____

5. At 10:30 p.m., I go to sleep.

   _____

6. At 12:00 a.m., I get up and eat a snack.

   _____

GRAMMAR FOCUS

ALL   MOST   SOME

3 A Read and answer.

1. Do some people eat potatoes for dinner?   *Yes, they do.*
2. Do most people sleep between 9:00 a.m. and 1:00 p.m.?   *No, they don't.*
3. Do some dogs read and write?   _____
4. Do all of the children in the United States play baseball?   _____
5. Do most people in Japan eat tomatoes for breakfast?   _____
6. Do all birds swim?   _____
7. Do most people sleep at night?   _____
8. Do some people eat lunch at 11:30 a.m.?   _____
9. Do all of the people in Canada go to bed before 11:00 p.m.?   _____
10. Do some children eat apples and bananas for a snack?   _____

Simple present   **33**

GRAMMAR FOCUS

Rosa eats lunch at 12:00 on Sunday, Monday, Tuesday, Wednesday, Thursday, Friday, and Saturday.	=	Rosa **always** eats lunch at 12:00.
Fernando eats lunch at 12:00 on Monday, Tuesday, Wednesday, Thursday, Friday, and Saturday.	=	Fernando **usually** eats lunch at 12:00.
Keiko eats lunch at 12:00 on Monday, Wednesday, and Friday.	=	Keiko **sometimes** eats lunch at 12:00.
Tarek eats lunch at 1:00 on Sunday, Monday, Tuesday, Wednesday, Thursday, Friday, and Saturday.	=	Tarek **never** eats lunch at 12:00.

4 A **Read and answer.**

1. I never drink water.   *False*
2. I always drink milk for breakfast.   _____
3. I usually wear shoes.   _____
4. I never wash my hands.   _____
5. I always eat good food.   _____
6. I usually read the newspaper.   _____
7. I sometimes eat butterflies for lunch.   _____
8. I never wear a hat.   _____
9. I usually listen to the radio in the car.   _____
10. I sometimes wash the car on Saturday. _____
11. I never write in English.   _____
12. I usually smile at my teacher.   _____
13. I sometimes drive to school.   _____
14. I never wear gloves in summer.   _____

Do you always wear sunglasses?
Do you usually wear sunglasses?
Do you sometimes wear sunglasses?   =   Do you **ever** wear sunglasses?
Do you never wear sunglasses?

4   **With a partner, ask and answer questions. Use *always*, *usually*, *sometimes*, or *never* in your answers.**

Juan: Maria, do you ever wear sunglasses?
Maria: Yes, I sometimes wear sunglasses.

1. Do you ever wear a hat?
2. Do you ever wear basketball shoes?
3. Do you ever eat a good breakfast?
4. Do you ever wear sandals?
5. Do you ever drive to school?
6. Do you ever wear gloves?
7. Do you ever play golf?
8. Do you ever drink hot water?
9. Do you ever wear a belt?
10. Do you ever listen to the radio?

often, every day
like, don't like

1 A   Listen.

A._____

B._____

C._____

D._____

E._____

F._____

G._____

H._____

I._____

J._____

K._____

L._____

1 B   Listen and write the letters.

1. ____
2. ____
3. ____

4. ____ ____
5. ____ ____
6. ____ ____

7. ____ ____ ____
8. ____ ____ ____
9. ____ ____ ____

GRAMMAR FOCUS

We eat cereal for breakfast Monday, Wednesday, Friday, and Saturday.	=	We **often** eat cereal for breakfast.
Linda **often** eats chicken for dinner. Linda **often** eats fish for dinner.	=	Linda **often** eats chicken or fish for dinner.

2 A   Read and answer.

1. In the United States, people often eat chocolate for breakfast.   *False*
2. In China, people often eat rice for dinner.   _____
3. In the United States, people often eat hamburgers and French fries for lunch.   _____
4. In Japan, people often eat carrots for breakfast.   _____
5. In Mexico, people often eat chicken and rice for dinner.   _____
6. In Colombia, people often eat peas and carrots for breakfast.   _____
7. In the United States, people often eat soup and a sandwich for lunch.   _____
8. In Canada, people often eat cereal and milk for breakfast.   _____
9. In the United States, people often eat beef and potatoes for dinner.   _____
10. In Brazil, people often eat chocolate eggs for lunch.   _____

2 B   Listen and answer.

Rosa always eats lunch at 12:00.   =   Rosa eats lunch at 12:00 **every day.**

3 Read and answer.

1. Do you drink water every day?   *Yes, I do.*
2. Do you eat lunch at the same time every day?   _____
3. Does the moon shine every night?   _____
4. Do you drive to school at the same time every day? _____
5. Do babies drink milk every day?   _____
6. Do you watch television every day?   _____
7. Does the sun set at the same time every day?   _____
8. Do you go to bed at the same time every night?   _____
9. Do you wear shoes every day?   _____
10. Do you wash your hands at the same time every day? _____
11. Do you watch the sun rise every day?   _____
12. Does it snow in Toronto every January?   _____

3 Listen and answer.

GRAMMAR FOCUS

I eat apples every day because I **like** apples.
I don't eat peas because I **don't like** peas.

4 Read and answer.

Emma likes carrots, corn, potatoes, cereal, bananas, chicken, fish, and milk.
Emma doesn't like peas, hamburgers, French fries, eggs, rice, and beef.

1. We're having cereal, milk, and bananas for breakfast.

    Emma will be happy. She likes cereal, milk, and bananas.

2. We're having hamburgers and French fries for lunch.

   Emma won't be happy. She doesn't like hamburgers and French fries.

3. We're having chicken and corn for dinner.

4. We're having eggs and rice for breakfast.

5. We're having carrot soup and fish sandwiches for lunch.

6. We're having fish, corn, and potatoes for dinner.

7. We're having beef sandwiches and pea soup for lunch.

4 **With a partner, tell what foods you like and don't like. Write sentences.**

Juan likes hamburgers, but he doesn't like chicken sandwiches.

LESSON 4

need to, want to

1 A Listen.

A._____

B._____

C._____

D._____

E._____

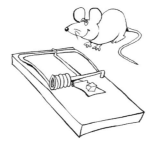

F._____

G._____

H._____

I._____

J._____

K._____

L._____

1 B Listen and write the letters.

1. ___
2. ___
3. ___
4. ___ ___

5. ___ ___
6. ___ ___
7. ___ ___
8. ___ ___

9. ___ ___ ___
10. ___ ___ ___
11. ___ ___ ___
12. ___ ___ ___

2 **A** Write. Use these words.

bug spray	a driver's license	a key	a knife	a match
money	a mousetrap	shampoo	a stamp	a telescope

1. What do we need to buy food?

   We need money.

2. What do we need to cut meat?

   _____

3. What do we need to mail a letter?

   _____

4. What do we need to catch a mouse?

   _____

5. What do we need to lock a door?

   _____

6. What do we need to burn paper?

   _____

7. What do we need to kill insects?

   _____

8. What do we need to see the stars?

   _____

9. What do we need to wash our hair?

   _____

10. What do we need to drive a car?

   _____

2 **B** With a partner, ask and answer the questions of 2A.

GRAMMAR FOCUS
Carla is hungry. She **wants to eat** a sandwich.

3   Read and write sentences. Use these words.

drink some water	eat some food	get a driver's license	get some medicine	go to the library
play tennis	see the stars	shower	sleep	wear her jacket

1. My nephew is tired.
   He wants to sleep.

2. My niece is hungry.
   _____

3. My aunt reads books every day.
   _____

4. My brothers are sick.
   _____

5. Eric has a new racket.
   _____

6. The dog is thirsty.
   _____

7. Grace has a new car.
   _____

8. My cousins are dirty.
   _____

9. My uncle has a new telescope.
   _____

10. My sister is cold.
   _____

4   Listen and put in 20 carets (^).

Bob: Hi, Jim. Is it true that you have a baby sister?

Jim: It sure is. Name is Peggy Ann.

Bob: I that name. Aren't those your names?

Jim: That's right. I an Aunt Peggy and an Aunt Ann.

Bob: How much Peggy Ann weigh?

Jim: 12 1/2 pounds. She all the time.

Bob: Well, that's what babies. They eat and.

Jim: Yes, and they.

Bob: She cry a lot?

Jim: She doesn't cry in the day, but night at midnight she. My father and mother hold her and then stops. But every time they her in bed she cries.

Bob: So do they do?

Jim: Well, they with her and they sing to her, but she stop.

Bob: Are parents tired?

Jim: Yes, they're exhausted! They don't go to bed the sun rises.

Write these words above the carets.

aunts'	before	cries	cry	do	does	does	doesn't	eats	every
have	her	like	new	play	put	she	sleep	what	your

5 **Find these words. Circle.**

TURN	RISE	SHINE	GROW
CIRCLE	BOUNCE	CLIMB	STRETCH
MELT	FREEZE	BURN	CATCH
LOCK	KILL		

```
L V G P K E H C L W N E M M T
Z O J T L G Y T S M S T V V A
Z X C C B B L T I I L C X T Q
V D R K A E R Q R S V L X Z U
R I P S M R P S R D Z I L C F
C E C P Q P B H Z I Q M R Z E
X S X Y B Z S R X W V B Q Q T
E V H K I L L T D X C C A A U
B D B I K J T H R C A T C H R
M O T A N G R O W E R F J A N
K C U T Z E L P P R T W U L T
J Q F N P R B T N L M C O L B
N R W B C F R E E Z E G H R W
Y N K K I E N G T X M K A F B
B U R N L C Y R S E K N Q E I
```

5 **With a partner, write the words you found in alphabetical order.**

bounce _____   _____

_____   _____

_____   _____

_____   _____

_____   _____

_____   _turn_ _____

Present continuous
Future with *will, going to*

present continuous

1 **A** **Listen.**

A._____

B._____

C._____

D._____

E._____

F._____

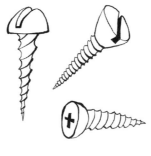

G._____

H._____

I._____

J._____

K._____

L._____

1 B Listen and write the letters.

1. ____   5. ____ ____   9. ____ ____ ____
2. ____   6. ____ ____   10. ____ ____ ____
3. ____   7. ____ ____   11. ____ ____ ____
4. ____   8. ____ ____   12. ____ ____ ____

1 C Spelling. Write the words on the blanks.

GRAMMAR FOCUS

| She has a flashlight in her right hand. | = | She's **holding** a flashlight in her right hand. |

---

2 A Look at the pictures and write.

1. _She's holding pliers in her left hand and a saw in her right hand._

2. _____

3. _____

4. _____

5. _____

6. _____

2 B With a partner, have a penny, a nickel, a dime, and a quarter. Hold two coins, one hidden in the right hand and one hidden in the left hand, and ask questions.

Maria: What am I holding in my left hand and in my right hand?

Juan: You're holding a penny in your left hand and a nickel in your right hand.

Maria: No, that's not right.

Juan: You're holding a nickel in your left hand and a dime in your right hand.

Maria :   Yes, you're right.

3 A Listen.

A._____

B._____

C._____

D._____

E._____

F._____

G._____

H._____

3 B Listen and write the letters.

1. ____

2. ____

3. ____

4. ____ ____

5. ____ ____

6. ____ ____

7. ____ ____ ____

8. ____ ____ ____

9. ____ ____ ____

3 C Spelling. Write the words on the blanks.

4   Write. Use these words.

hammering and sawing	driving in the sun	cooking	exercising	sleeping
listening to music	riding a motorcycle	standing in the rain	swimming	

1. People wear sweat suits when   *they're exercising.*
2. People wear aprons when _____
3. People wear helmets when _____
4. People wear raincoats when _____
5. People wear earphones when _____
6. People wear pajamas when _____
7. People wear safety glasses when _____
8. People wear swimsuits when _____
9. People wear sunglasses when _____

GRAMMAR FOCUS

Questions	Answers
What is your name?	My name is Maria Hernandez.
Is New York an American city?	Yes, New York is an American city.

5   Read and answer.

1. Are you eating a green apple?   *No, I'm not.*
2. Are you wearing blue clothes? _____
3. Are you holding a paper clip in your left hand? _____
4. Are you writing with a pencil? _____
5. Are you holding a pencil or pen in your hand? _____
6. Are you learning Chinese? _____
7. Are you holding money in your hand? _____
8. Are you answering questions? _____
9. Are you sitting on a chair? _____
10. Are you holding a newspaper in your mouth? _____

5   Listen and answer.

1 A Listen.

A._____

B._____

C._____

D._____

E._____

F._____

G._____

H._____

I._____

J._____

1 B Listen and write the letters.

1. ____

2. ____

3. ____

4. ____

5. ____ ____

6. ____ ____

7. ____ ____

8. ____ ____ ____

9. ____ ____ ____

10. ____ ____ ____

1 C Spelling. Write the words on the blanks.

hammer/saw   hammering/sawing

2 Write answers. Use these words.

cooking food	cutting hair	flying an airplane	taking photographs
hammering and sawing	painting a house	planting a tree	
repairing a car	serving food	sweeping the floor	

1. What's the custodian doing?

   He's sweeping the floor.

2. What are the gardeners doing?

   They're planting a tree.

3. What's the beautician doing?

   _____

4. What are the chefs doing?

   _____

5. What's the pilot doing?

   _____

6. What are the waiters doing?

   _____

7. What's the mechanic doing?

   _____

8. What are the painters doing?

   _____

9. What are the construction workers doing?

   _____

10. What's the photographer doing?

    _____

GRAMMAR FOCUS

John is cold.
He's going to **put on** his jacket.

John is warm.
He's going to **take off** his jacket.

3 | **Write. Use these words.**

apron	belt	clean clothes	glasses	gloves
helmet	pajamas	safety glasses	sweat suit	swimsuit

1. What is Ann going to do before she cooks dinner?

   She's going to put on her apron.

2. What is Miguel going to do after he saws and hammers?

   He's going to take off his safety glasses.

3. What is Fernando going to do before he rides his motorcycle?

   _____

4. What are the children going to do before they go to bed?

   _____

5. What is Rosa going to do before she goes to the gym?

   _____

6. What is Ming going to do after he goes swimming?

   _____

7. What is Bill's grandfather going to do before he reads the newspaper?

   _____

8. What is Yung Sun going to do before he digs in the garden?

   _____

9. What is Carla going to do after she showers?

   _____

10. What is Miguel going to do after he puts on his pants?

   _____

VOCABULARY FOCUS

I need to write a letter but I don't have a pen. Can I **borrow** your pen?

4 Write sentences. Use these words.

burn some wood	catch a mouse	cut the sandwich	cut the paper
hammer and saw	kill some insects	lock the door	mail some letters
plant some flowers	sweep the floor	take some pictures	wash my hair

1. Can I borrow your camera?
   I need to take some pictures.

2. Can I borrow your broom?

3. Can I borrow a knife?

4. Can I borrow your spade?

5. Can I borrow your key?

6. Can I borrow a mousetrap?

7. Can I borrow your scissors?

8. Can I borrow some matches?

9. Can I borrow some shampoo?

10. Can I borrow your bug spray?

11. Can I borrow some stamps?

12. Can I borrow your safety glasses?

LESSON 3

will
if . . . , what time . . . ?

1 **Listen.**

A._____

B._____

C._____

D._____

E._____

F._____

G._____

H._____

I._____

J._____

K._____

L._____

1 **Listen and write the letters.**

1. ____   5. ____   9. ____ ____
2. ____   6. ____   10. ____ ____
3. ____   7. ____ ____   11. ____ ____ ____
4. ____   8. ____ ____   12. ____ ____ ____

1 **Spelling. Write the words on the blanks.**

VOCABULARY FOCUS
begin = start
end = finish = be done
go to sleep = begin sleeping
wake up = end sleeping

2   Read and answer.

1. If Linda leaves at 3:00 and drives for four hours, what time will she arrive?

   She'll arrive at 7:00.

2. If Miguel starts to study at 7:30 and studies for two hours, what time will he be done?

   _____

3. If Bill turns on the radio at 11:00 and listens for three hours, what time will he turn it off?

   _____

4. If the plane takes off at 10:00 a.m. and flies for two hours, what time will it arrive?

   _____

5. If Carla and Emma go to sleep at midnight and sleep for 10 hours, what time will they wake up?

   _____

6. If the movie begins at 6:30 and lasts for one and a half hours, what time will it end?

   _____

7. If Pablo and Ann turn on the television at 5:00 and watch it for one half hour, what time will they turn it off?

   _____

8. If it starts to rain at noon and rains for 12 hours, what time will it stop?

   _____

9. If Tarek gets in the water at 9:15 and swims for 45 minutes, what time will he get out?

   _____

10. If Rosa begins to paint at 6:30 and paints for two and a half hours, what time will she finish?

    _____

11. If Fernando starts at 9:00 and works for eight hours, what time will he finish?

    _____

3 Read and answer.

1. If you drop eggs, will they break?   *Yes, they will.*
2. If you burn paper, will it melt?   *No, it won't.*
3. If you water flowers, will they grow?   _____
4. If you heat water, will it freeze?   _____
5. If you drop a tennis ball, will it bounce? _____
6. If you kiss babies, will they smile?   _____
7. If you heat ice, will it melt?   _____
8. If you drop a hammer in the ocean, will it float? _____
9. If you brush your teeth, will they turn green? _____
10. If you hammer your glasses, will they break? _____

3 Listen and answer.

GRAMMAR FOCUS	
Singular	**Plural**
The flower grows.	The flowers grow.

4 Write. Use these words.

bounce   break   burn   grow   lock   melt   melt   smile

1. We heat ice.
   When we heat ice, it melts.
2. We drop eggs.
   When we drop eggs, they break.
3. We water flowers.
   _____
4. We kiss babies.
   _____
5. We drop tennis balls.
   _____
6. We close our door.
   _____

7. We hold a match to paper.

_____

8. We hold snowballs in our warm hands.

_____

5 | **Find these words. Circle.**

HAMMER	NAILS	SAW	WRENCH
NUTS	BOLTS	SCREWDRIVER	SCREWS
PLIERS	DRILL	FLASHLIGHT	

```
N  A  I  L  S  F  D  O  A  Y  D  Y  Z  H  V
Z  W  X  L  Y  S  H  V  J  U  S  F  C  C  J
H  J  Q  U  G  E  Q  U  N  S  C  A  J  F  V
F  L  A  S  H  L  I  G  H  T  T  T  W  R  X
C  P  C  X  H  U  P  T  A  W  O  T  E  H  L
S  C  R  E  W  D  R  I  V  E  R  M  O  L  L
W  H  M  S  R  R  E  W  S  N  M  G  I  B  W
S  R  E  D  L  P  I  J  U  A  R  R  L  O  M
T  V  I  R  A  H  B  T  H  N  D  T  M  L  G
O  Q  O  W  V  G  N  N  W  H  S  A  A  T  B
P  L  I  E  R  S  D  U  B  H  Z  Q  Y  S  Z
T  R  S  D  P  O  G  M  T  L  L  R  O  P  A
U  N  T  W  R  E  N  C  H  S  Q  Y  E  P  X
M  M  Z  B  A  C  Y  D  P  M  P  S  G  J  N
P  V  D  Z  G  Y  S  S  C  R  E  W  S  P  B
```

5 | **With a partner, write the words you found in alphabetical order.**

bolts _____   _____

_____   _____

_____   _____

_____   _wrench_ _____

_____

Girl: Mama, it 6:00?
Mama: No, yet. It's 5:45.

Girl: Mama, is 6:00?
Mama: No, not yet. 5:50.

Girl: Mama, is it?
Mama: No, not. It's 5:57.

Girl: Mama, is it 6:00 yet?

Mama: Yes, now 6:00.

Girl: We go in now?

Mama: Yes, now we can in.

Girl: What time is the movie going start?

Mama: 6:30.

Girl: Can I some popcorn and a soda before it starts?

Mama: Yes.

Girl: Can I have a big box popcorn and a big soda?

Mama: No, that's much.

Girl: I have some chocolate candy?

Mama: No, it isn't good eat too much.

Girl: Mama?

Mama: Yes?

Girl: Is it yet?

Mama: No, not yet. It's.

6 B Write these words above the carets.

6:00 6:10 6:30 at can can go have is it it's it's not of to to too yet

5 | Past tense

was/were
how old?

1 A Listen.

Abraham Lincoln

Sun Yat-sen

A._____

William Shakespeare

Jane Austen

B._____

Pablo Picasso

Leonardo da Vinci

C._____

Ludwig van Beethoven

Giacomo Puccini

D._____

Marie Curie

Albert Einstein

E._____

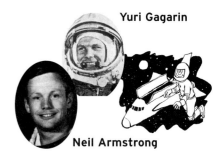

Yuri Gagarin

Neil Armstrong

F._____

1 B Listen and write the letters.

1. ____
2. ____
3. ____

4. ____ ____
5. ____ ____
6. ____ ____

7. ____ ____
8. ____ ____ ____
9. ____ ____ ____

1 Spelling. Write the words on the blanks.

2 Read and answer.

1. Were Beethoven and Puccini composers?   _Yes_
2. Was Pablo Picasso an artist?   _____
3. Was Neil Armstrong an American president?   _____
4. Were Albert Einstein and Marie Curie scientists?   _____
5. Was Shakespeare an astronaut?   _____
6. Were Picasso and Leonardo da Vinci artists?   _____
7. Was Yuri Gagarin an astronaut?   _____
8. Was Sun Yat-sen a Chinese president?   _____
9. Was Beethoven a scientist?   _____
10. Was Jane Austen a writer?   _____

2 Listen and answer.

GRAMMAR FOCUS

BEETHOVEN
1770-1827

Beethoven was born in 1770.
He died in 1827.

Listen and write the dates.

1. Beethoven was born in _1770_ and died in _1827_ .
2. Shakespeare was born in _____ and died in _____.
3. Lincoln was born in _____ and died in _____.
4. Sun Yat-sen was born in _____ and died in _____.
5. Marie Curie was born in _____ and died in _____.
6. Puccini was born in _____ and died in _____.
7. Leonardo da Vinci was born in _____ and died in _____.
8. Yuri Gagarin was born in _____ and died in _____.
9. Jane Austen was born in _____ and died in _____.
10. Picasso was born in _____ and died in _____.
11. Einstein was born in _____ and died in _____.
12. Neil Armstrong was born in _____.

GRAMMAR FOCUS		
What is your age? I am 20 years old.	=	How old are you? I am 20 years old.

3 B **Write.**

1. How old was Picasso when he died?

   He was 92 years old.

2. How old were Beethoven and Puccini when they died?

   Beethoven was 57 years old, and Puccini was 66 years old.

3. How old were Lincoln and Sun Yat-sen when they died?

   _____

4. How old was Jane Austen when she died?

   _____

5. How old were Leonardo da Vinci and Picasso when they died?

   _____

6. How old was Shakespeare when he died?

   _____

7. How old was Marie Curie when Albert Einstein was born?

   _____

8. How old was Neil Armstrong when Yuri Gagarin was born?

_____

9. How old was Picasso when Puccini died?

_____

10. How old was Beethoven when Jane Austen died?

_____

4 **With a partner, ask and answer questions.**

How old were you when your younger brother/sister was born?
How old was your older brother/sister when you were born?

Maria: How old were you when your younger brother was born?

Juan: I was 10 years old.

          OR

Juan: I don't have any younger brothers.

GRAMMAR FOCUS	
Singular	**Plural**
There wasn't any soup.	There weren't any carrots.

5 **Write. Use these words.**

chocolate   cold   hot   in English   red   yellow

1. Why didn't you get some soup?

Because there wasn't any that was hot.

2. Why didn't she buy some bananas?

_____

3. Why didn't he buy some books?

_____

4. Why didn't they drink some milk?

_____

5. Why didn't she buy some tomatoes?

_____

6. Why didn't he buy some candy?

_____

past tense *-ed* vs. *-d*
why, but, because

1 A **Listen.**

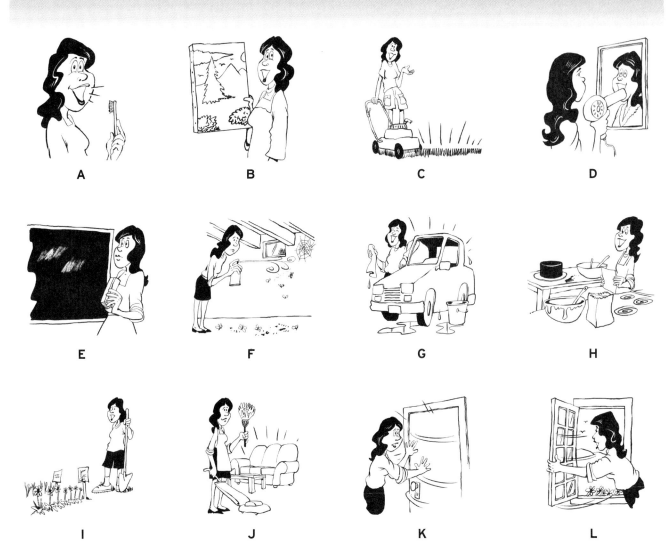

1 B **Listen and write the letters.**

1. ____   5. ____   9. ____ ____

2. ____   6. ____   10. ____ ____ ____

3. ____   7. ____ ____   11. ____ ____ ____

4. ____   8. ____ ____   12. ____ ____ ____

1   Read and answer.

1. Sophie baked a cake.   _A_
2. Sophie brushed her teeth.   _____
3. Sophie cleaned her room.   _____
4. Sophie closed the door.   _____
5. Sophie dried her hair.   _____
6. Sophie erased the board.   _____
7. Sophie killed some insects.   _____
8. Sophie mowed the grass.   _____
9. Sophie opened the window.   _____
10. Sophie painted a picture.   _____
11. Sophie planted some flowers.   _____
12. Sophie washed her car.   _____

2   Read and answer.

1. Sophie painted her teeth.   _False_
2. Sophie mowed the grass.   _____
3. Sophie killed some insects.   _____
4. Sophie burned the cake.   _____
5. Sophie opened the window.   _____
6. Sophie erased a picture.   _____
7. Sophie dried her hair.   _____
8. Sophie washed her car.   _____
9. Sophie cleaned her room.   _____
10. Sophie cooked some flowers.   _____

2   Listen and answer.

GRAMMAR FOCUS

We go to see our grandmother.	=	We visit our grandmother.

3 Write.

1. We usually wash the car on Saturday,   (week / Friday)
   but last week we washed it on Friday.

2. We usually fish in the summer,   (year / January)
   but last year we fished in January.

3. We usually paint the house in August,   (year / September)
   _____

4. We usually telephone our aunt on Wednesday,   (week / Thursday)
   _____

5. We usually visit our cousins in Colombia in May,   (year / April)
   _____

6. We usually cook fish and rice for dinner on Monday,   (week / Tuesday)
   _____

7. We usually plant new trees in the spring,   (year / autumn)
   _____

8. We usually mow the grass on Friday,   (week / Thursday)
   _____

GRAMMAR FOCUS

Present			Past
cook	+ed	=	cooked
paint			painted
play			played
erase	+d	=	erased
shave			shaved
close			closed
cry	-y + ied	=	cried
dry			dried

4 A   Spelling. Write the words on the blanks.

1. _closed_
2. _____
3. _____
4. _____
5. _____
6. _____
7. _____
8. _____
9. _____
10. _____

4 B   Write. Use the words of 4A.

1. You ____opened____ the window because the room was hot.
2. We _____ the door with a key.
3. We mixed black and white paint and _____ the house gray.
4. She _____ at everybody yesterday because she was happy.
5. When he _____ the hot match, he burned his finger.
6. You _____ your hands with soap and water.
7. The baby _____ because he was hungry.
8. They _____ to play soccer but they didn't have a ball.
9. She _____ the window because it started to rain.
10. After class the teacher _____ the board.

1 A **Look at the back cover and listen to the colors.**

1 B **Read and answer.**

1.	Do red and white make pink?	*Yes, they do.*
2.	Do black and white make gray?	_____
3.	Do blue and white make green?	_____
4.	Do red and yellow make brown?	_____
5.	Do green and black make blue?	_____
6.	Do brown and white make tan?	_____
7.	Do red and blue make purple?	_____
8.	Do blue and white make dark blue?	_____
9.	Do yellow and blue make green?	_____
10.	Do white and yellow make light yellow?	_____

1 C **Listen and answer.**

Write sentences.

1. gray   *When we mix black and white, we make gray.*
2. pink   _____
3. purple   _____
4. tan   _____
5. light blue   _____
6. orange   _____
7. green   _____
8. dark blue   _____

2   **Read and write.**

1. She wanted to paint her car pink,   *so she mixed red and white paint.*
2. He wanted to paint his door light blue, _____
3. Rosa and I wanted to paint a room green, _____
4. My niece wanted to paint her desk purple, _____
5. Our uncle wanted to paint a table orange, _____
6. Our aunt wanted to paint a bookcase light yellow, _____

GRAMMAR FOCUS

He had some nails.	He **had** a hammer.
He didn't have any nails.	He **didn't have** a hammer.

---

3   **Write. Use these words.**

baseballs	basketball	driver's license	hammer	match
nuts and bolts	paints	pencils	piano	racket

1. I didn't have a car, but   *I had a driver's license.*
2. I had some pens, but   *I didn't have any pencils.*
3. She didn't have any nails, but _____
4. He had a bat, but _____
5. He didn't have any tennis balls, but _____
6. They had some wood, but _____
7. We didn't have any music, but _____
8. He had a brush, but _____
9. We had five players, but _____
10. She had a wrench, but _____

GRAMMAR FOCUS

I have two books. One of the books is on the desk and the **other** book is on the table.

4 Listen and put in 18 carets (˄).

Our grandmother born in 1899, and she died in 1998. She was almost 100 years old when she. She cooked and cleaned day, but she was also a very good artist. She to sit next to a big window, listen to music by Beethoven, and pictures of her family. She had grandchildren, and she to paint pictures of them. My cousin Catherine was older the other grandchildren, so she painted her. Everybody was older than I was, so she painted me. When she started painting picture the only paints she had blue, white, and black. She painted me in blue, blue, and dark blue. I the picture very much. I like it more than any picture she ever painted. My grandmother my painting "Grandma's Picasso" because Picasso painted many pictures blue.

4 Write these words above the carets.

all	died	eleven	every	first	in	last	light	like
liked	my	named	other	paint	than	wanted	was	were

5 Find these words. Circle.

ASTRONAUT	GARDENER	COMPOSER	MECHANIC
ARTIST	PAINTER	BEAUTICIAN	CUSTODIAN
WRITER	PRESIDENT	CHEF	WAITER
SCIENTIST	PHOTOGRAPHER		

```
Q  C  O  F  K  W  T  K  A  B  S  C  I  I  N
K  Q  O  S  V  S  E  Z  K  E  C  H  L  W  V
G  N  Y  M  I  V  T  B  T  A  I  E  D  H  P
M  K  C  T  P  R  I  E  D  U  E  F  X  C  O
U  E  R  U  Y  O  N  B  R  T  N  G  Z  B  P
C  A  C  N  S  D  S  E  B  I  T  A  Q  F  R
U  R  A  H  M  T  T  E  M  C  I  R  P  T  E
U  W  H  S  A  I  O  G  R  I  S  D  W  U  S
T  S  E  T  A  N  N  D  T  A  T  E  R  X  I
K  R  V  W  M  P  I  C  I  N  E  N  I  Q  D
A  P  S  K  U  F  M  C  L  A  A  E  T  T  E
K  C  W  P  A  I  N  T  E  R  N  R  E  B  N
P  H  O  T  O  G  R  A  P  H  E  R  R  C  T
X  A  H  L  K  V  D  H  T  C  M  B  W  M  E
X  A  S  T  R  O  N  A  U  T  W  V  E  K  H
```

5 B With a partner, write the words you found in alphabetical order.

artist _____   *mechanic* _____

_____   _____

_____   _____

_____   _____

_____   _____

_____   _____

6 Review

1   **Look at the pictures. Circle the sentence.**

1.   **A.** Jim is washing the car.
       B. Jim washed the car.
       C. Jim is going to wash the car.

2.   **A.** Jim mailed a letter.
       B. Jim will mail a letter.
       C. Jim didn't mail a letter.

3.   **A.** These birds can fly.
       B. These birds can't fly.
       C. These birds can't swim.

4.   **A.** Jim is playing tennis.
       B. Jim will play tennis.
       C. Jim can't play tennis.

5.   **A.** A snowman doesn't melt when it's hot.
       B. A snowman can't melt when it's hot.
       C. A snowman always melts when it's hot.

6.   **A.** Jim erased the board.
       B. Jim is erasing the board.
       C. Jim isn't able to erase the board.

2 Write sentences. Use these words.

a stamp	a driver's license	a key	a telescope	a match
a mousetrap	some bread and meat	some bug spray	some helmets	some soap

1. Bill wants to mail a letter.

   Well, if he wants to mail a letter, he'll need a stamp.

2. Rosa wants to catch a mouse.

   _____

3. Miguel's sister wants to lock the door.

   _____

4. The girls want to see the stars.

   _____

5. My brother wants to wash his hands.

   _____

6. Her father wants to kill some insects.

   _____

7. My sister wants to drive the car.

   _____

8. Keiko's brothers want to ride motorcycles.

   _____

9. My grandmother wants to burn the wood.

   _____

10. Steve and Laura want to eat some sandwiches.

    _____

3 Look at the form. Write these words on the blanks.

apartment number	city	date of birth	first name	last name	state
middle initial	signature	street address	telephone number	Zip Code	

Miller   Sara   C.   January 4, 1971

1. _last name_   2. _____   3. _____   4. _____

1514 Lincoln Street   #27

5. _____   6. _____

San Francisco   CA   90000

7. _____   8. _____   9. _____

415-454-2570

10. _____

Sarah C. Miller

11. _____

4 A Listen to the telephone conversation and put in 20 carets (∧).

Mrs. Edwards:	Hello.
Kim:	Hello, Mrs. Edwards. This Kim Johnson. Is Cindy home?
Mrs. Edwards:	Just a minute, Kim. I'll call. – Cindy, Kim Johnson on the phone.
Cindy:	Hi, Kim. You study your math?
Kim:	Yes, I studied it dinner. But after dinner Rob called, and he me to go to the basketball game him on Friday. Is it okay with you if I go with you and Sara?
Cindy:	Everybody that you like Rob. It's okay.
Kim:	You sure?
Cindy:	It's okay. We'll ask Carlos and Mark to go with. We can all meet the game.
Kim:	Oh, we going to the game our school. We're going the game at Rob's school.
Cindy:	Well, okay, I . . .
Kim:	And I one other question. Can I borrow dark blue skirt?
Cindy:	But, Kim, you already have light blue sweater. You borrowed that week.
Kim:	Yes, I know. But I need your light blue sweater to with your dark blue skirt.

4 B Write these words above the carets.

are	aren't	asked	at	at	before	did	don't	have	her
is	it's	knows	last	my	to	us	wear	with	your

LESSON 1

kind of
ate, drank, saw

1 A Listen.

A._____

B._____

C._____

D._____

E._____

F._____

G._____

H._____

I._____

J._____

K._____

L._____

1 B   Listen and write the letters.

1. ___   6. ___ ___
2. ___   7. ___ ___
3. ___ ___   8. ___ ___ ___
4. ___ ___   9. ___ ___ ___
5. ___ ___   10. ___ ___ ___

1 C   Spelling. Write the words on the blanks.

2 A   Read and answer.

1. Are apples a kind of fruit?   *Yes*
2. Is butter a kind of meat?   _____
3. Are oranges a kind of vegetable?   _____
4. Is cheese a kind of dairy product?   _____
5. Are carrots a kind of vegetable?   _____
6. Is corn a kind of dessert?   _____
7. Is ham a kind of meat?   _____
8. Are bananas a kind of fruit?   _____
9. Is milk a kind of dairy product?   _____
10. Is cake a kind of dessert?   _____

2 B   Listen and answer.

GRAMMAR FOCUS	
Present	**Past**
eat	ate
drink	drank

2 C   Read and write.

Roger likes carrots, beef, oranges, cake, cheese, carrot juice, orange juice, and milk.

Roger doesn't like peas, chicken, bananas, pies, butter, tomato juice, apple juice, and soda.

1. What kind of meat did Roger eat?

   He ate beef, but he didn't eat chicken.

2. What kind of drink did Roger drink?

   He drank milk, but he didn't drink soda.

3. What kind of dairy products did Roger eat?

   _____

4. What kind of fruit did Roger eat?

   _____

5. What kind of fruit juice did Roger drink?

   _____

6. What kind of vegetable did Roger eat?

   _____

7. What kind of dessert did Roger eat?

   _____

8. What kind of vegetable juice did Roger drink?

   _____

GRAMMAR FOCUS	
Present	**Past**
see	saw

3 A   Class activity. Look at the money and classroom objects.

3 B   With a partner, write what you saw.

We saw two pennies.

_____

_____

_____

_____

_____

_____

_____

4 **Write. Use these words.**

boots	brother	butterflies	car	cows
ducks	nails	stars	sunset	wrench

1. Did you see the moon last night?
   No, but I saw the stars.

2. Did you see Mary's sister yesterday?
   _____

3. Did you see the bees on the flowers?
   _____

4. Did you see the horses eating grass?
   _____

5. Did you see Steve's new shoes?
   _____

6. Did you see the sunrise?
   _____

7. Did you see his uncle's new truck?
   _____

8. Did you see the chickens?
   _____

9. Did you see the screws?
   _____

10. Did you see the pliers?
    _____

1 A Read and answer.

1. Do you know how to write the alphabet? _____*Yes*_____
2. Do you know how to drive a car? _____
3. Do you know how to fly an airplane? _____
4. Do you know how to play soccer? _____
5. Do you know how to bake a cake? _____
6. Do you know how to turn on a computer? _____
7. Do you know how to cook elephant meat? _____
8. Do you know how to play the piano? _____
9. Do you know how to read Chinese books? _____
10. Do you know how to skate on ice? _____

1 B Listen and answer.

GRAMMAR FOCUS	
Present	**Past**
know how to	knew how to

2 A Read and answer.

1820-1895

Bill's great-great-grandmother
What did she know how to do?

1. She knew how to cook chicken. _____*True*_____
2. She knew how to drive a car. _____*False*_____
3. She knew how to ride a horse. _____

4. She knew how to sew.   _____

5. She knew how to fly an airplane.   _____

6. She knew how to wash clothes.   _____

7. She knew how to send e-mails.   _____

8. She knew how to sweep floors.   _____

9. She knew how to cook food in a microwave. _____

10. She knew how to plant flowers.   _____

2 B Listen and answer.

GRAMMAR FOCUS	
Present	**Past**
Can Paul play football today?	**Could** Paul play football yesterday?
No, he can't. It's raining.	No, he **couldn't**. It was raining.

3 A Write. Use these words.

burn the paper	buy any new clothes	drive the car	mail the letter
open the door	plant the tree	read the book	
see the planets	wash my hands	write the letter	

1. I didn't have a key, _so I couldn't open the door._

2. I didn't have a match, _____

3. I didn't have a driver's license, _____

4. I didn't have a pen or pencil, _____

5. I didn't have a spade, _____

6. I didn't have a stamp, _____

7. I didn't have any soap and water, _____

8. I didn't have a telescope, _____

9. I didn't have any money, _____

10. I didn't have my glasses, _____

1. _Because she didn't have a key._
2. _____
3. _____
4. _____
5. _____
6. _____

4 **Read and circle.**

1. There were two books. One was in English, and one was in Chinese. Which one could Bill read?

   (The one that was in English.)   The one that was in Chinese.

2. There were two balls. One was a baseball, and one was a basketball. Which one could Bill bounce?

   The one that was a baseball.   The one that was a basketball.

3. There were two letters. One was with a stamp, and one was without a stamp. Which one could Bill mail?

   The one that was with a stamp.   The one that was without a stamp.

4. There were two chickens. One was cooked, and one was not cooked. Which one could Bill eat?

   The one that was cooked.   The one that was not cooked.

5. There were two shirts. One was wet, and one was dry. Which one could Bill put on?

   The one that was wet.   The one that was dry.

6. There were two names. One was on the board, and one was erased. Which one could Bill read?

   The one that was on the board.   The one that was erased.

7. There were two houses. One cost $50,000, and one cost $5 million. Which one could Bill buy?

   The one that cost $50,000.   The one that cost $5 million.

8. There were two spiders. One was under the bed, and one was on the bed. Which one could Bill see?

   The one that was under the bed.   The one that was on the bed.

Listen and put in 18 carets (ꞈ).

Lisa's grandmother and grandfather vegetarians. They ate meat. When she went to their house for Sunday dinner, they rice, vegetables, cheese, fruit, salads, and eggs. For dessert they usually ate apple or other fruit, but sometimes they ice cream. Lisa's grandparents drank water, and vegetable juice. They tomato juice, so they often tomato juice they ate dinner. They never drank tea or coffee, and they never drank cola or any of soda. Her grandparents knew how cook good meals meat. Lisa ate all her food at their house because was so good. Today, Lisa's grandchildren come to house for dinner. She cooks good meals with and rice just like the meals she ate her grandparents' house.

Write these words above the carets.

always	an	at	ate	before	drank	had	her	it	kind
liked	milk	never	them	to	vegetables	were	without

Read and answer.

1. Lisa's grandparents never ate cheese. _____*False*_____
2. Her grandparents never drank coffee. _____
3. Her grandparents always ate ice cream for dessert. _____
4. Lisa and her grandparents drank tomato juice before they ate dinner. _____
5. Lisa's grandparents often drank soda after dinner. _____
6. Her grandparents knew how to cook good meals without meat. _____
7. Lisa and her grandparents usually ate fruit for dessert. _____
8. Lisa liked to eat dinner at her grandparents' house. _____
9. Lisa's grandparents ate cheese, but they didn't eat eggs. _____
10. Today, Lisa never cooks meals with rice. _____

Listen and answer.

if . . . , must
have to

1 **A** **Listen.**

A._____

B._____

C._____

D._____

E._____

F._____

G._____

H._____

I._____

J._____

1. ___   6. ___ ___
2. ___   7. ___ ___
3. ___   8. ___ ___ ___
4. ___ ___   9. ___ ___ ___
5. ___ ___   10. ___ ___ ___

1 C Spelling. Write the words on the blanks.

2 Write. Use these words.

be at the airport before noon	climb slowly	cook it
have a cell phone	have a computer	have a driver's license
have a library card	have a razor	have an umbrella
put on a jacket	run fast	study every night

1. If you want to drive a car, *you must have a driver's license.*
2. If you want to win the race, _____
3. If you want to be a good student, _____
4. If you want to borrow books from the library, _____
5. If you want to eat the meat, _____
6. If you want to shave, _____
7. If you don't want to be cold, _____
8. If you want to telephone from a train, _____
9. If you don't want to fall, _____
10. If you want to send e-mails, _____
11. If you want to fly to Chicago, _____
12. If you don't want to be wet, _____

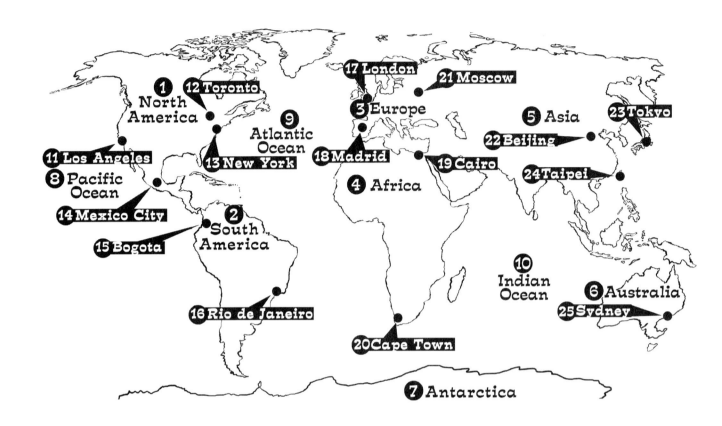

VOCABULARY FOCUS

go from New York to Los Angeles = **cross** the United States

must cross = **have to** cross

1. To go from New York to London, we have to cross the Atlantic Ocean. _True_
2. To go from Tokyo to Cairo, we have to cross the Indian Ocean. _____
3. To go from Moscow to Taipei, we have to cross the Pacific Ocean. _____
4. To go from Australia to Africa, we have to cross the Indian Ocean. _____
5. To go from Rio de Janeiro to Madrid, we have to cross Europe. _____
6. To go from Sydney to Cape Town, we have to cross Australia and Asia. _____
7. To go from London to Beijing, we have to cross Europe and Asia. _____
8. To go from Cape Town to Rio de Janeiro, we have to cross the Pacific Ocean. _____
9. To go from Toronto to Bogota, we have to cross the Pacific Ocean. _____
10. To go from Cairo to Mexico City, we have to cross Africa and the Atlantic Ocean. _____

3 | **Look at the map and write.**

1. Bill was in New York, and he wanted to go to London.
   He had to cross the Atlantic Ocean.
2. Bill was in Taipei, and he wanted to go to Moscow.

   _____
3. Bill was in Cape Town, and he wanted to go to Cairo.

   _____
4. Bill was in Toronto, and he wanted to go to Madrid.

   _____
5. Bill was in Rio de Janeiro, and he wanted to go to Mexico City.

   _____
6. Bill was in Sydney, and he wanted to go to Cape Town.

   _____
7. Bill was in Moscow, and he wanted to go to Tokyo.

   _____
8. Bill was in London, and he wanted to go to Los Angeles.

   _____

4 **Write. Use these words.**

cell phone	computer	driver's license	key	library card
money	paddle	racket	scissors	shampoo

1. What will Wendy have to have to play tennis?

    She'll have to have a racket.

2. What will Wendy have to have to drive a car?

   _____

3. What will Wendy have to have to wash her hair?

   _____

4. What will Wendy have to have to buy a gift?

   _____

5. What will Wendy have to have to send e-mails?

   _____

6. What will Wendy have to have to get a library book?

   _____

7. What will Wendy have to have to lock the door?

   _____

8. What will Wendy have to have to cut the paper?

   _____

9. What will Wendy have to have to play Ping-Pong?

   _____

10. What will Wendy have to have to telephone from a train?

   _____

4 **Listen and answer.**

CARROTS	**VEGETABLES**	**CAKE**	**MEAT**
CHEESE	**DESSERT**	**JUICE**	**FRUIT**
BEEF	**MILK**	**BUTTER**	**ORANGES**

```
F  V  F  A  J  R  Y  N  I  S  J  U  I  C  E
V  O  A  C  E  C  M  H  E  I  L  E  D  L  M
F  S  T  T  F  S  K  L  V  Q  O  R  O  S  F
P  U  T  E  A  O  B  O  R  A  N  G  E  S  R
E  U  E  J  C  A  C  C  K  R  V  F  P  C  U
B  B  A  J  T  S  E  G  G  A  R  O  D  H  I
D  J  Y  E  C  A  R  R  O  T  S  E  W  E  T
A  X  G  F  P  Q  A  G  A  A  S  A  F  E  K
A  E  M  C  L  I  D  M  X  S  V  D  V  S  A
V  D  A  J  W  W  E  E  E  J  K  K  U  E  M
B  K  U  T  H  P  L  E  S  M  D  R  J  D  N
C  A  K  E  Z  A  T  Y  E  S  K  W  J  J  G
R  C  V  H  T  R  F  Y  I  K  E  V  H  H  G
L  K  M  E  A  T  X  M  I  L  K  R  A  W  L
N  G  X  G  Q  R  Q  I  S  P  P  J  T  O  U
```

5 B **With a partner, write the words you found in alphabetical order.**

beef _____   _____

_____   _____

_____   _____

_____   _____

_____

8 Comparatives, superlatives

comparatives, superlatives
adjectives of size

1 Listen.

1. Pacific Ocean – _____ square miles
2. Mississippi River – _____ miles
3. Amazon River – _____ miles
4. Atlantic Ocean – _____ square miles
5. Sahara Desert – _____ square miles
6. Nile River – _____ miles
7. Mt. Kilimanjaro – _____ feet

8. Kalahari Desert – _____ square miles
9. Africa – _____ square miles
10. Indian Ocean – _____ square miles
11. Gobi Desert – _____ square miles
12. Mt. Everest – _____ feet
13. Asia – _____ square miles
14. Mt. Fuji – _____ feet
15. Australia – _____ square miles

1 B Read and answer.

1. Which is higher, Mt. Everest or Mt. Fuji? _Mt. Everest_

2. Which is larger, the Atlantic Ocean or the Pacific Ocean? _____

3. Which is longer, the Amazon River or the Nile River? _____

4. Which is smaller, Africa or Asia? _____

5. Which is higher, Mt. Kilimanjaro or Mt. Fuji? _____

6. Which is larger, the Indian Ocean or the Atlantic Ocean? _____

7. Which is longer, the Mississippi River or the Amazon River? _____

8. Which is larger, the Gobi Desert or the Kalahari Desert? _____

1 C Write.

1. Nile River / Amazon River
   The Nile River is longer than the Amazon River.

2. Kalahari Desert / Sahara Desert
   _____

3. Mt. Kilimanjaro / Mt. Fuji
   _____

4. Indian Ocean / Atlantic Ocean
   _____

5. Amazon River / Mississippi River
   _____

6. Mt. Everest / Mt. Kilimanjaro
   _____

2 A Listen.

A._____

B._____

C._____

D._____

E._____

F. the _____

2 B Listen and write the letters.

1. ____
2. ____
3. ____
4. ____ ____

5. ____ ____
6. ____ ____
7. ____ ____
8. ____ ____ ____

2 C Spelling. Write the words on the blanks.

GRAMMAR FOCUS

Mt. Fuji is 12,388 feet high. Mt. Fuji is a **high** mountain.

Mt. Kilimanjaro is 19,340 feet high. Mt. Kilimanjaro is a **higher** mountain.

Mt. Everest is 29,035 feet high. Mt. Everest is the **highest** mountain in the world.

1. What is the largest continent in the world?   *Asia* _____
2. What is the longest river in the world?   _____
3. What is the largest ocean in the world?   _____
4. What is the smallest continent in the world?   _____
5. What is the highest mountain in Africa?   _____
6. What is the longest river in South America?   _____
7. What is the coldest continent in the world?   _____
8. What is the largest desert in the world?   _____
9. What is the highest mountain in Japan?   _____
10. What is the largest desert in East Asia?   _____

3 B Listen and answer.

4 Write.

1. There isn't any river in the world longer than the Nile.
   The Nile is the longest river in the world.

2. There isn't any continent in the world larger than Asia.
   _____

3. There isn't any desert in the world larger than the Sahara.
   _____

4. There isn't any ocean in the world larger than the Pacific.
   _____

5. There isn't any mountain in the world higher than Mt. Everest.
   _____

6. There isn't any continent in the world colder than Antarctica.
   _____

7. There isn't any mountain in Africa higher than Mt. Kilimanjaro.
   _____

8. There isn't any river in South America longer than the Amazon.
   _____

9. There isn't any continent in the world smaller than Australia.
   _____

10. There isn't any desert in East Asia larger than the Gobi.
    _____

comparatives, superlatives
descriptive adjectives

GRAMMAR FOCUS

Singular	Plural
person	people

1 A Listen.

A._____ people

B._____ people

C. a _____ person

D. a _____ person

E._____ people

F._____ people

G. a _____ person

H. a _____ person

I. a _____ driver

J. a _____ driver

K. a _____ fruit

L. a _____ fruit

M. a _____ dog

N. a _____ dog

O. a _____ room

P. a _____ room

1. ____   5. ____ ____   9. ____ ____ ____
2. ____   6. ____ ____   10. ____ ____ ____
3. ____   7. ____ ____   11. ____ ____ ____
4. ____ ____   8. ____ ____   12. ____ ____ ____

1 **Spelling. Write the words on the blanks.**

2 **Read and write.**

1. He is a person who gives money to poor people.
   He is a good person.

2. They are dogs that the children like.
   They are nice dogs.

3. They are people who don't have any money.
   _____

4. She is a person who needs some medicine.
   _____

5. It is a room that is painted black.
   _____

6. They are people who wear very large clothes.
   _____

7. He is a person who never needs medicine.
   _____

8. They are drivers who drive too fast.
   _____

9. It is a fruit that people don't like to eat.
   _____

10. They are people who have a large house and many big cars.
    _____

GRAMMAR FOCUS

heavy   heavier   heaviest

1. Our father sometimes smiles.
   Our grandfather always smiles.
   Our mother usually smiles.
   (happy)

   Our father is happy.
   Our mother is happier than our father.
   Our grandfather is the happiest of the three.

2. Her grandmother has $2 million.
   Her uncle has $4 million.
   Her aunt has $1 million.
   (rich)

3. The tennis player can lift 200 pounds.
   The football player can lift 290 pounds.
   The baseball player can lift 215 pounds.
   (strong)

4. A race horse can run 40 mph.
   An African cat can run 70 mph.
   A deer can run 45 mph.
   (fast)

5. His sister has $2.
   His cousin doesn't have any money.
   His brother has $5.
   (poor)

6. Our brother is 6 months old.
   Our sister is 2 years old.
   Our cousin is 3 weeks old.
   (young)

more, most
good, well
good/well, better, best

GRAMMAR FOCUS

Put the book in Bill's hands. = **Give** Bill the book.

1 **Write. Use these words.**

books	flowers	food	gifts	gloves
money	notebooks and pencils	umbrellas	water	medicine

1. What do we give people when they are sick?
   We give them medicine.

2. What do we give our children when they are hungry?
   _____

3. What do we give our mothers on Mother's Day?
   _____

4. What do we give our dogs when they are thirsty?
   _____

5. What do we give our children when it is raining?
   _____

6. What do we give our students when they first go to school?
   _____

7. What do we give our children when they need to buy new clothes?
   _____

8. What do we give our parents on their birthdays?
   _____

9. What do we give our children when they want to read?
   _____

10. What do we give our children when their hands are cold?
    _____

1 **Class activity.**

Give your book to the student on your right.

Teacher: Juan gave his book to Paul. Is that true?
Maria: Yes, it's true.
Teacher: Paul gave his book to Maria. Is that true?
Juan: No, he gave it to Kim.

1 C With a partner, write sentences.

Juan gave his book to Paul.
We gave our books to Maria and Kim.

GRAMMAR FOCUS		
money	**more** money	**the most** money

TABLE OF MEASUREMENTS

1 kilo = 2.2 pounds	12 inches = 1 foot	1 quart = 2 pints
1 pound = 16 ounces	3 feet = 1 yard	1 gallon = 8 pints
		3 teaspoons = 1 tablespoon

2 A Read and write.

1. I gave Sara 3 dimes and a nickel.

   I gave Miguel 3 nickels and 10 pennies.

   I gave Mary 2 quarters and a dime.

   Sara has more money than Miguel, but Mary has the most money.

2. We gave John 4 quarters and 2 dimes.

   We gave Paul 8 dimes and 4 nickels.

   We gave Anna 10 nickels and a quarter.

   _____

3. Eric gave Carla 3 quarts of milk.

   Eric gave Laura 5 pints of milk.

   Eric gave Steve 1 gallon of milk.

   _____

4. They gave Mike 2 pounds of bananas.

   They gave Allison 1 pound, 12 ounces of bananas.

   They gave Jenny 1 kilo of bananas.

   _____

5. Louis gave Grace 4 feet of paper.
   Louis gave Nina 2 yards of paper.
   Louis gave Ann 5 feet, 10 inches of paper.

   _____

6. Jane gave Pete 3 tablespoons of rice.
   Jane gave Don 3 teaspoons of rice.
   Jane gave Rob 1 tablespoon and 3 teaspoons of rice.

   _____

2 B **Class Activity. In groups of three fill in the charts. Write sentences.**

NAME	AUNTS & UNCLES
Juan	5
Paul	4
Maria	8

Juan has more aunts and uncles than Paul, but Maria has the most.

NAME	AUNTS & UNCLES		NAME	BROTHERS & SISTERS
____	_____		____	_____
____	_____		____	_____
____	_____		____	_____

NAME	COUSINS		NAME	NIECES & NEPHEWS
____	_____		____	_____
____	_____		____	_____
____	_____		____	_____

GRAMMAR FOCUS

He is a good writer. = He writes **well**.

bounces	burns	cuts	drives	flies	runs	shaves	writes

1. It's a good knife.

   Yes, it cuts well.

2. It's a good basketball.

   _____

3. It's a good pen.

   _____

4. It's a good candle.

   _____

5. It's a good razor.

   _____

6. It's a good airplane.

   _____

7. It's a good car.

   _____

8. It's a good horse.

   _____

3 B | **Listen and answer.**

GRAMMAR FOCUS		
good	better	the best

4 | **Write sentences.**

1. We can read what Tom is writing. We can't read what Rob is writing.

   Tom writes better than Rob.

2. We like how Lisa is singing. We don't like how Beth is singing.

   _____

3. We won't eat what Joe is cooking. We will eat what Mike is cooking.

   _____

4. We can't wear the clothes that Ed is sewing. We can wear the clothes that Mark is sewing.

_____

5. We will ride in the car that Lisa is driving. We won't ride in the car that Brad is driving.

_____

6. We listen when Ann is reading. We don't listen when David is reading.

_____

5 Write. Use these words.

artist	beautician	chef	composer	construction worker
custodian	gardener	mechanic	photographer	waiter

1. Nobody in Beijing could cook better than his uncle.

Yes, he was the best chef in China.

2. Nobody in Los Angeles could clean better than his nephew.

_____

3. Nobody in Tokyo could take pictures better than my aunt.

_____

4. Nobody in Paris could cut hair better than their niece.

_____

5. Nobody in Rio de Janeiro could plant trees better than her brother.

_____

6. Nobody in Madrid could serve food better than our son.

_____

7. Nobody in Chicago could repair cars better than her husband.

_____

8. Nobody in Bogota could hammer and saw better than his sister.

_____

9. Nobody in New York could paint pictures better than our mother.

_____

10. Nobody in Toronto could write music better than their daughter.

_____

When my Aunt Ruth young, she went around the world. She crossed the Ocean to Europe, and then she went to Asia. Asia is the largest, and there was a lot to. She saw the Gobi Desert and the highest in the world, Mt. Everest. After Asia she went to to see the longest river the world, the Nile. Then she crossed largest desert, the Sahara. Next, she went by airplane to the continent in the, Antarctica. From Antarctica, she went to Australia, the world's continent. From Australia, she crossed the ocean in the world, the Pacific. It took her months to go to all those places. When she got home, she said, "I the world's highest mountain, the river, the coldest continent, and the desert. But now that I am home, I the happiest person in the world."

6 B   Write these words above the carets.

Africa	am	Atlantic	coldest	continent	first
hottest	in	largest	longest	mountain	saw
see	six	smallest	the	was	world

6 C   Read and answer.

1. Aunt Ruth was old when she went around the world.   *False*
2. First, she crossed the Atlantic Ocean to Europe.   _____
3. When she was in Asia, she saw Mt. Everest.   _____
4. Before she went to Africa, she saw the longest river in the world.   _____
5. In Africa, she crossed the largest desert.   _____
6. She went by airplane to the coldest continent.   _____
7. She went from Antarctica to Australia.   _____
8. From Australia, she crossed the smallest ocean, the Pacific.   _____
9. Aunt Ruth didn't go to South America.   _____
10. She was not happy to be home.   _____

6 D   Listen and answer.

SWEETEST	**COLDEST**	**HIGHEST**	**LONGEST**
HAPPIEST	**LARGEST**	**HEAVIEST**	**NICEST**
OLDEST	**YOUNGEST**	**HOTTEST**	**SMALLEST**

```
Y  H  S  K  T  B  O  T  H  O  T  T  E  S  T
E  O  C  W  K  S  S  T  S  E  I  Y  A  E  L
Q  D  U  X  E  E  E  A  C  S  S  D  J  N  O
X  T  O  N  I  E  O  G  M  O  H  M  U  I  N
U  N  S  P  G  N  T  G  R  G  L  R  L  D  G
E  X  P  E  F  E  L  E  C  A  V  D  N  Y  E
T  A  M  B  C  L  S  A  S  L  Y  F  E  E  S
H  S  D  G  E  I  L  T  O  T  F  V  N  S  T
H  F  E  S  T  X  N  N  O  T  G  G  W  L  T
I  O  T  P  H  S  M  A  L  L  E  S  T  A  U
G  P  C  B  G  E  V  Q  K  Z  N  J  D  R  Z
H  J  X  D  S  I  W  U  N  U  S  E  T  G  H
E  L  F  T  K  X  H  O  L  D  E  S  T  E  B
S  N  I  C  E  S  T  D  L  A  Q  P  L  S  M
T  U  S  H  E  A  V  I  E  S  T  X  T  T  D
```

7 **With a partner, write the words you found in alphabetical order.**

coldest _____ _____

_____ _____

_____ _____

_____ _____

_____ _____

1   Listen.

A._____

B._____

C._____

D._____

E._____

F._____

G._____

H._____

I._____

J._____

K._____

L._____

1   Listen and write the letters.

1. ____
2. ____
3. ____
4. ____ ____

5. ____ ____
6. ____ ____
7. ____ ____ ____
8. ____ ____ ____

9. ____ ____ ____
10. ____ ____ ____
11. ____ ____ ____
12. ____ ____ ____

1   Spelling. Write the words on the blanks.

2   Listen.

A._____

B._____

C._____

D._____

E._____

F._____

2   Listen and write the letters.

1. ____
2. ____
3. ____

4. ____ ____
5. ____ ____
6. ____ ____

7. ____ ____
8. ____ ____ ____
9. ____ ____ ____

2   Spelling. Write the words on the blanks.

3 A Read and answer.

1. Is the sofa in the kitchen?   *No*

2. Is the dresser in the bedroom?   _____

3. Is the microwave in the garage?   _____

4. Is there a lamp in the living room?   _____

5. Are there some dishes in the cabinets? _____

6. Is the stove in the living room?   _____

7. Are there armchairs in the bathroom? _____

8. Is the microwave above the stove?   _____

9. Are there some tools in the dining room? _____

10. Is the refrigerator in the kitchen?   _____

11. Is there furniture in the garage?   _____

12. Are there some towels in the bathroom? _____

3 B Listen and answer.

4 A Write. Use these words.

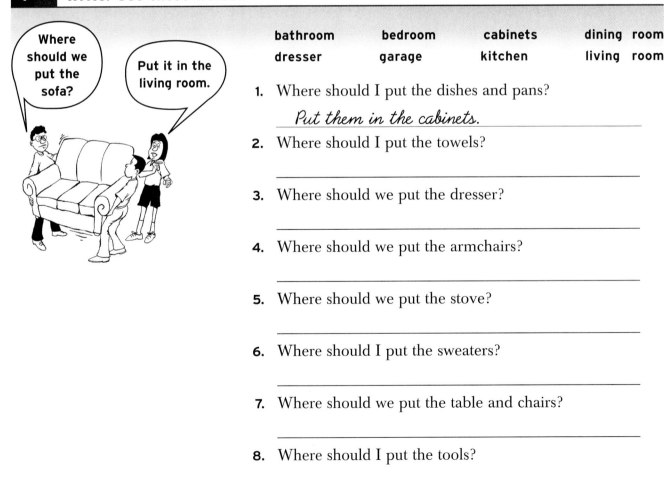

bathroom	bedroom	cabinets	dining room
dresser	garage	kitchen	living room

1. Where should I put the dishes and pans?

   Put them in the cabinets.

2. Where should I put the towels?

   _____

3. Where should we put the dresser?

   _____

4. Where should we put the armchairs?

   _____

5. Where should we put the stove?

   _____

6. Where should I put the sweaters?

   _____

7. Where should we put the table and chairs?

   _____

8. Where should I put the tools?

GRAMMAR FOCUS
When your hands are dirty, it is good to wash them.
When your hands are dirty, you **should** wash them.

5 A Write. Use these words.

buy a stamp	give them milk	go to sleep	put on safety glasses	cook it
put on jackets	put on helmets	open a window	take some medicine	dry it

1. What should we do before we ride a motorcycle?
   We should put on helmets.

2. What should we do when we are sick?
   _____

3. What should we do when babies cry?
   _____

4. What should we do when we are cold?
   _____

5. What should we do before we hammer and saw?
   _____

6. What should we do when we are tired?
   _____

7. What should we do when our hair is wet?
   _____

8. What should we do when the room is hot?
   _____

9. What should we do before we eat the meat?
   _____

10. What should we do before we mail a letter?
   _____

5 B Listen and answer.

past continuous

 1 A Listen.

A._____

B._____

C._____

D._____

E._____

F._____

G._____

H._____

I._____

J._____

K._____

L._____

 1 B Listen and write the letters.

1. ____

2. ____

3. ____

4. ____ ____

5. ____ ____

6. ____ ____

7. ____ ____ ____

8. ____ ____ ____

9. ____ ____ ____

10. ____ ____ ____

1 C Spelling. Write the words on the blanks.

2 A Write. Use these words.

hair dryer	hose	knife	match	mower
scale	scissors	tape measure	vacuum cleaner	pen

1. What do we use to cut meat?

    We use a knife.

2. What do we use to dry our hair?

    _____

3. What do we use to light a candle?

    _____

4. What do we use to measure the window?

    _____

5. What do we use to cut paper?

    _____

6. What do we use to wash the car?

    _____

7. What do we use to clean the rug?

    _____

8. What do we use to write our names?

    _____

9. What do we use to weigh the apples?

    _____

10. What do we use to cut the grass?

    _____

2 B Listen and answer.

3 A Write. Use these sentences.

I climbed the tree.	I locked the door.
I cooked some vegetables.	I saw some microbes.
I cut the sandwiches.	I sewed some clothes.
I dried my hands.	I washed the car.
I killed the insects.	I weighed the potatoes.

1. I used the key.   *I locked the door.*
2. I used the hose.   _____
3. I used the pan.   _____
4. I used the towel.   _____
5. I used the needle.   _____
6. I used the ladder.   _____
7. I used the knife.   _____
8. I used the microscope.   _____
9. I used the bug spray.   _____
10. I used the scale.   _____

3 B With a partner, write sentences from 3A.

1. *That is the key I used to lock the door.*
2. *That is the hose I used to wash the car.*
3. _____
4. _____
5. _____
6. _____
7. _____
8. _____
9. _____
10. _____

4 A Write answers.

1. What were the chefs using to cut the meat?

    They were using a knife.

2. What was Keiko using to dry her hair?

    She was using a hair dryer.

3. What was Pablo using to light the fire?

_____

4. What was Sam using to cut the grass?

_____

5. What were Kim and Sara using to weigh the baby?

_____

6. What was Bill using to wash the car?

_____

7. What was Carla using to measure the window?

_____

8. What were James and Mary using to cook the vegetables?

_____

9. What was John using to climb the tree?

_____

10. What was Sophie using to clean the rug?

_____

4 ▪ Listen and answer.

1 **A** **Listen and repeat the cities.**

GRAMMAR FOCUS	
Present	**Past**
go	went

1 B Read and answer.

1. We went from Mexico City to Miami. Did we go northeast? <u>Yes</u>
2. We went from Chicago to Houston. Did we go southwest? _____
3. We went from Vancouver to San Francisco. Did we go north? _____
4. We went from Los Angeles to New York. Did we go northeast? _____
5. We went from Montreal to Atlanta. Did we go southeast? _____
6. We went from Houston to Miami. Did we go northeast? _____
7. We went from Chicago to Vancouver. Did we go northwest? _____
8. We went from New York to Mexico City. Did we go southwest? _____
9. We went from Los Angeles to Montreal. Did we go northeast? _____
10. We went from Atlanta to San Francisco. Did we go southwest? _____

1 C Answer. Use these words.

north	northeast	northwest	southwest	southwest	west

1. We went from San Francisco to Vancouver. Which direction did we go?

    We went north.

2. We went from Atlanta to Los Angeles. Which direction did we go?

   _____

3. We went from Montreal to New York. Which direction did we go?

   _____

4. We went from Chicago to Mexico City. Which direction did we go?

   _____

5. We went from Miami to San Francisco. Which direction did we go?

   _____

6. We went from Houston to Atlanta. Which direction did we go?

   _____

1 D Class Activity. Follow directions.

Teacher: Juan, go to the window.
            Maria, go to the door.

Teacher: Who went to the door?
Paul: Maria went to the door. (Maria did.)

GRAMMAR FOCUS

| The student is studying English. | = | The student is **learning** English. |

2 A **Write. Use these words.**

| cook food | cut hair | fly an airplane | grow flowers | paint pictures |
| repair cars | serve food | speak English | use a computer | write music |

1. What can we learn from the English teacher?

   We can learn how to speak English.

2. What can we learn from the pilot?

   _____

3. What can we learn from the chef?

   _____

4. What can we learn from the mechanic?

   _____

5. What can we learn from the artist?

   _____

6. What can we learn from the beautician?

   _____

7. What can we learn from the computer science teacher?

   _____

8. What can we learn from the gardener?

   _____

9. What can we learn from the waiter?

   _____

10. What can we learn from the composer?

    _____

2 B **With a partner, ask and answer the questions of 2A.**

GRAMMAR FOCUS

What can we learn from English teachers?	=	What can English teachers **teach** us?

Present		**Past**
teach		taught

2 C Write sentences.

1. What did the waiters teach you?

   They taught us how to serve food.

2. What did the mechanics teach you?

   _____

3. What did the artists teach you?

   _____

4. What did the pilots teach you?

   _____

5. What did the chefs teach you?

   _____

6. What did the computer science teachers teach you?

   _____

7. What did the gardeners teach you?

   _____

8. What did the beauticians teach you?

   _____

9. What did the English teachers teach you?

   _____

10. What did the composers teach you?

   _____

2 D Listen and answer.

Listen and put in 17 carets (ᴧ).

Tom: Did sister like the lamp I her for her new apartment?

Lisa: Yes, she liked a lot. She said it looked good with her furniture.

Tom: Where she put it?

Lisa: I think she put it in the living behind her sofa. That was very nice of you to give that lamp.

Tom: Well, I . . .

Lisa: You know, Tom, I you like my sister.

Tom: Well, I . . .

Lisa: You are asking about her.

Tom: Yes, well, I think she really nice.

Lisa: That's what she saying about you. She said, "Tom is really a person."

Tom: She did? Did she that?

Lisa: I'm to see her tonight. I say to her that you like her?

Tom: Well, I don't know you should say that. But . . . you say that I think she's really nice.

---

3 B **Write these words above the carets.**

always	can	did	gave	going	her	if	is	it
new	nice	room	say	should	think	was	your	

---

3 C **Read and answer.**

1. Tom gave a lamp to Lisa's sister.   _True_

2. Lisa's sister liked the lamp.   _____

3. Her sister put the lamp under the sofa.   _____

4. Lisa thinks Tom likes her sister.   _____

5. Tom said he didn't like Lisa's sister.   _____

6. Lisa's sister said that Tom was really nice.   _____

7. Lisa and Tom are going to see her sister.   _____

8. Tom wants Lisa to say to her sister that he likes her.   _____

9. Lisa thinks Tom should go to see her sister.   _____

10. Tom thinks that Lisa's sister is really nice.   _____

---

3 D **Listen and answer.**

Find these words. Circle.

STOVE	**REFRIGERATOR**	**DRESSER**	**CABINETS**
FURNITURE	**PANS**	**KITCHEN**	**SOFA**
MICROWAVE	**FREEZER**	**LAMP**	**GARAGE**
ARMCHAIR	**DISHES**		

```
D I S H E S L C Z E E G I G L
W O K W S Z A A E M G E Q A D
M A O P Q C M B X V J A F R R
I E R Z J D P I E T O H R A E
C B Y M U I I N W B S O F G F
R X F M C G R E G U I R S E R
O E E R I H N T U G I F B E I
W I V M E E A S K G E U R G G
A P F A H E S I E N D R G M E
V K A C W K Z R R B E N Z S R
E A T N M O A E P W G I X T A
Z I K C S T R H R K L T A O T
K W D M O H X C X U X U Y V O
M H L R S O F A L M G R X E R
D R E S S E R B U M Q E D Y L
```

With a partner, write the words you found in alphabetical order.

armchair

_____   _____

_____   _____

_____   _____

_____   _____

_____   _____

_____   _____

10 Present perfect

would
keep/kept
find/found

 1 A Listen.

A._____

B._____

C._____

D._____

E._____

F._____

G._____

H._____

I._____

 1 B Listen and write the letters.

1. ____   4. ____ ____   7. ____ ____ ____
2. ____   5. ____ ____   8. ____ ____ ____
3. ____   6. ____ ____   9. ____ ____ ____

1 C Spelling. Write the words on the blanks.

VOCABULARY FOCUS

| He never gives money to anyone. | = | He always **keeps** all of his money. |

2 A Read and answer.

1. Linda usually keeps her tools in a tool box.   <u>True</u>
2. Linda usually keeps her clothes in a closet.   _____
3. Linda usually keeps her hammers and screwdrivers in her jewelry box.   _____
4. Linda usually keeps her credit cards in her wallet.   _____
5. Linda usually keeps her rings in her kitchen cabinets.   _____
6. Linda usually keeps her dictionary in a bookcase.   _____
7. Linda usually keeps her tools in her dresser.   _____
8. Linda usually keeps her money in her purse.   _____
9. Linda usually keeps her jewelry box in the garage.   _____
10. Linda usually keeps her bracelets and necklaces in a pan.   _____

2 B Listen and answer.

GRAMMAR FOCUS

If you give me some chocolate, I will eat it.

If you gave me some chocolate, I **would** eat it.

3 A Read and circle the answer.

1. If Bill gave Linda a ring, where would she keep it?
   (in her jewelry box)   in her tool box
2. If Bill gave Linda a wallet, where would she keep it?
   in her closet   in her purse
3. If Bill gave Linda some socks, where would she keep them?
   in her kitchen cabinets   in her dresser
4. If Bill gave Linda a saw and a tape measure, where would she keep them?
   in her purse   in her tool box
5. If Bill gave Linda a dictionary, where would she keep it?
   in her dresser   in her bookcase
6. If Bill gave Linda some dishes, where would she keep them?
   in her kitchen cabinets   in her closet
7. If Bill gave Linda a tool box, where would she keep it?
   in the bathroom   in the garage
8. If Bill gave Linda some pens and pencils, where would she keep them?
   in her jewelry box   in her desk

3   Listen and answer.

GRAMMAR FOCUS	
Present	**Past**
keep	kept

4   Write. Use these words.

books	clothes	desserts	fruit
furniture	jewelry	money	tools

1. Did they give you a dictionary?
   No, they kept all the books.

2. Did they give you a wrench?
   _____

3. Did they give you a shirt?
   _____

4. Did they give you a ring?
   _____

5. Did they give you an apple?
   _____

6. Did they give you a dollar?
   _____

7. Did they give you a pie?
   _____

8. Did they give you a chair?
   _____

GRAMMAR FOCUS	
Present	**Past**
write	wrote

5   Class Activity. Write your address on a piece of paper. Answer questions.

Teacher:	10 Lincoln Street. Who **wrote** this?
Student:	I **wrote** that.

VOCABULARY FOCUS

I can't **find** my wallet. = I don't know where my wallet is.

6 A Write. Use these words.

bathroom cabinet	bookcase	closet	desk	dresser
jewelry box	kitchen cabinets	purse	tool box	wallet

1. I can't find my jacket.

   It should be in my closet, but it isn't.

2. I can't find my rings.

   They should be in my jewelry box, but they aren't.

3. I can't find my hammer.

   _____

4. I can't find my credit cards.

   _____

5. I can't find my pans.

   _____

6. I can't find my keys.

   _____

7. I can't find my red pen.

   _____

8. I can't find my dictionary.

   _____

9. I can't find my towels.

   _____

10. I can't find my socks.

   _____

GRAMMAR FOCUS

Present	Past
find	fouund

6 B Class Activity. Before class, hide some pens, pencils, coins, keys, etc. around the classroom. Ask your classmates to find them. Answer questions.

Teacher: Who **found** the red pen?

Student 1:   I **found** it.

Teacher: Who **found** the keys?

Student 2:   I **found** them.

GRAMMAR FOCUS

man

men

woman

women

1900

1 A Read and answer.

1. In 1900, American women always wore long skirts.   *True*
2. In 1900, American men usually wore shorts.   _____
3. In 1900, American women always wore sandals.   _____
4. In 1900, American women often wore hats.   _____
5. In 1900, American men sometimes wore sweaters.   _____
6. In 1900, American women usually wore jeans.   _____
7. In 1900, American men never wore hats.   _____
8. In 1900, American women often wore T-shirts.   _____
9. In 1900, American women sometimes wore gloves.   _____
10. In 1900, American men and women usually wore contact lenses.   _____

1 B Listen and answer.

2 Write. Use these words.

caps	contact lenses	jeans and sweaters	T-shirt
sandals	short	short skirts	

1. Women in 1900 always wore long skirts, but *women today often wear short skirts.*
2. People in 1900 often wore glasses, but _____
3. Men in 1900 often wore hats, but _____
4. Men in 1900 often wore suits, but _____
5. Men and women in 1900 always wore shoes or boots, but _____
6. Men in 1900 usually wore shirts, but _____
7. Women in 1900 usually wore their hair long, but _____

3   **Listen.**

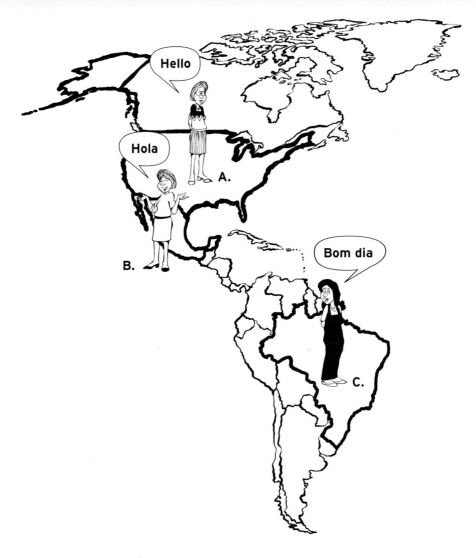

3   **Listen and write the letters.**

1. ____
2. ____
3. ____
4. ____
5. ____ ____

6. ____ ____
7. ____ ____
8. ____ ____ ____
9. ____ ____ ____
10. ____ ____ ____

3   **Write the letter.**

1. Arabic _____ *E*
2. Chinese _____
3. English _____

4. French _____
5. Japanese _____
6. Korean _____

7. Portuguese _____
8. Russian _____
9. Spanish _____

3 **D** **Read and answer.**

1. Do the people in France speak French? _Yes, they do._
2. Do the people in Brazil speak English? _No, they don't._
3. Do the people in Korea speak Russian? _____
4. Do the people in Egypt speak Arabic? _____
5. Do the people in the United States speak English? _____
6. Do the people in Mexico speak Spanish? _____
7. Do the people in China speak Chinese? _____
8. Do the people in Mexico speak Portuguese? _____
9. Do the people in Russia speak Russian? _____
10. Do the people in Brazil speak Portuguese? _____

3 E Listen and answer.

GRAMMAR FOCUS	
Present	**Past**
speak	spoke

4 A Write. Use these words.

Brazil	Canada	China	Egypt	France
Japan	Korea	Mexico	Russia	the United States

1. Her uncle spoke French to her.

   That's right. He is from France.

2. His grandmother spoke Japanese to him.

   _____

3. Her cousins spoke English to her.

   _____

4. His niece spoke Spanish to him.

   _____

5. Their grandfather spoke Korean to them.

   _____

6. His aunts spoke Arabic to him.

   _____

7. Our grandparents spoke Chinese to us.

   _____

8. Her nephews spoke Portuguese to her.

   _____

9. His sister spoke Russian to him.

   _____

10. Our parents spoke French and English to us.

   _____

4 B Listen and answer.

> **GRAMMAR FOCUS**
>
> Abraham Lincoln was born in 1809 and died in 1865.
> Abraham Lincoln **lived** from 1809 to 1865.
> Abraham Lincoln **lived** in the United States.

5 | Read and answer.

1. Abraham Lincoln lived in the United States.
   What language did he speak?

   He spoke English.

2. Yuri Gagarin lived in Russia.
   What language did he speak?

   _____

3. Marie Curie lived in France.
   What language did she speak?

   _____

4. Jane Austen lived in England.
   What language did she speak?

   _____

5. Pablo Picasso lived in Spain and France.
   What languages did he speak?

   _____

6. Sun Yat-sen lived in China and the United States.
   What languages did he speak?

   _____

7. President Anwar Sadat lived in Egypt.
   What language did he speak?

   _____

8. Artist Lucio Costa lived in Brazil.
   What language did he speak?

   _____

5 | Listen and answer.

LESSON 3

make/made

 1 **A** **Listen.**

A._____

B._____

C._____

D._____

E._____

F._____

G._____

H._____

I._____

 1 **B** **Listen and write the letters.**

1. ____   4. ____ ____   7. ____ ____ ____
2. ____   5. ____ ____   8. ____ ____ ____
3. ____   6. ____ ____   9. ____ ____ ____

1 **C** **Spelling. Write the words on the blanks.**

2 Write. Use these words.

beans and peppers	bread and meat	bread	flour and fruit	beef
tomatoes	lettuce and tomatoes	milk	vegetables and meat	flour

1. What do people use to make sandwiches?

   They use bread and meat.

2. What do people use to make salads?

   _____

3. What do people use to make cheese?

   _____

4. What do people use to make soup?

   _____

5. What do people use to make ketchup?

   _____

6. What do people use to make chili?

   _____

7. What do people use to make bread?

   _____

8. What do people use to make hamburgers?

   _____

9. What do people use to make toast?

   _____

10. What do people use to make pies?

   _____

2 Listen and answer.

My family and I ˍ to a small town in Illinois where you ˍ see how people lived in the 1800s. In those days, most ˍ the people didn't ˍ a lot of money. They couldn't buy things, ˍ they made what they needed. My family and I saw how they ˍ soap, and we ˍ how they made candles. We saw a man who was making horseshoes, and we saw women who ˍ making clothes.

In those days, ˍ got up at sunrise, and they worked all day. We saw the ˍ of food they ate. They didn't ˍ hamburgers, French fries, or pizza. They usually ate some kind of ˍ with potatoes and some kind of vegetable. They usually went to bed ˍ 9:00 p.m.

Abraham Lincoln lived in ˍ town. We saw the post office where he worked. He was a ˍ man in those days. He liked to read. He read ˍ book that he could borrow. The people in the town didn't ˍ that he was ˍ to be president of the United States.

3 **B** **Write these words above the carets (ˍˍˍ).**

before	could	eat	every	going	have	kind	know	made
meat	of	people	saw	so	this	went	were	young

3 **C** **Read and answer.**

1. In Illinois, there is a small town where Abraham Lincoln lived. _True_
2. The family saw how people made soap and candles. _____
3. Some people knew how to make horseshoes. _____
4. The family saw some women who were making clothes. _____
5. The people in the 1800s ate pizza and French fries. _____
6. They usually went to bed before 9:00 p.m. and they got up before midnight. _____
7. Abraham Lincoln worked in a post office. _____
8. He knew how to read, but he couldn't borrow any books. _____
9. The people in the town knew he was going to be president. _____
10. The family saw the books that Abraham Lincoln read. _____

4 **A** **Find these words. Circle.**

MADE	DRANK	WROTE	KEPT
WERE	ATE	SPOKE	TAUGHT
SAW	WENT	FOUND	GAVE
WORE	KNEW		

```
W  J  G  H  O  O  Z  P  U  Q  M  W  U  K  J
S  O  G  L  E  W  X  I  N  N  A  Y  N  J  L
P  E  R  V  G  S  E  D  D  T  D  A  W  Z  V
V  Y  F  E  S  T  F  N  O  R  E  M  E  X  J
D  R  F  U  W  R  G  U  T  N  A  Z  R  H  C
R  U  X  J  S  R  N  V  I  C  M  I  E  S  S
O  T  O  M  S  D  O  Z  M  C  K  O  T  Z  A
X  S  O  N  P  D  O  T  G  D  C  T  O  E  W
H  A  U  L  O  Y  R  Y  E  Q  Y  L  O  L  P
D  K  G  E  K  K  I  A  O  C  E  O  J  I  P
C  Q  E  E  E  L  T  N  N  T  A  U  G  H  T
D  A  V  K  U  G  W  F  J  K  M  P  D  N  K
Q  A  Q  H  E  J  G  U  E  F  O  U  N  D  R
G  W  P  H  P  Y  Y  Z  K  N  E  W  O  N
K  I  Y  L  L  Y  T  C  F  W  V  N  A  T  E
```

4 **B** **With a partner, write the words you found in alphabetical order.**

ate _____   _____

_____   _____

_____   _____

_____   _____

_____   _____

11 Relative clauses

question tags
bought, sold

 1 A Listen.

A. a _____ of milk

B. a _____ of bread

C. a _____ of soup

D. a _____ of lettuce

E. a _____ of eggs

F. a _____ of jam

G. a _____ of soda

H. a _____ of flour

I. a _____ of cereal

J. a _____ of cheese

K. a _____ of soap

L. a _____ of paper towels

1. ___   5. ___ ___   9. ___ ___ ___

2. ___   6. ___ ___   10. ___ ___ ___

3. ___   7. ___ ___   11. ___ ___ ___

4. ___   8. ___ ___   12. ___ ___ ___

1 C **Spelling. Write the words on the blanks.**

2 A **Read and circle.**

1. Did they buy a pound of eggs or a carton of eggs?

   a pound of eggs   (a carton of eggs)

2. Did they buy a can of soup or a bottle of soup?

   a can of soup   a bottle of soup

3. Did they buy a bag of flour or a box of flour?

   a bag of flour   a box of flour

4. Did they buy a jar of soda or a bottle of soda?

   a jar of soda   a bottle of soda

5. Did they buy a head of lettuce or a pound of lettuce?

   a head of lettuce   a pound of lettuce

6. Did they buy a gallon of soap or a bar of soap?

   a gallon of soap   a bar of soap

7. Did they buy a roll of paper towels or a box of paper towels?

   a roll of paper towels   a box of paper towels

8. Did they buy a pound of cheese or a bag of cheese?

   a pound of cheese   a bag of cheese

9. Did they buy a loaf of bread or a pound of bread?

   a loaf of bread   a pound of bread

10. Did they buy a can of cereal or a box of cereal?

    a can of cereal   a box of cereal

2 B **Listen and answer.**

VOCABULARY FOCUS		GRAMMAR FOCUS	
mother = mom		**Present**	**Past**
father = dad		buy	bought

3 A **Write. Use these words.**

bag	bar	bottle	box	can	carton
gallon	head	jar	loaf	pound	roll

1. Sam's dad bought some flour, didn't he?

   Yes, he bought a bag of flour.

2. Sam's mom bought some bread, didn't she?

   _____

3. Sam's dad bought some lettuce, didn't he?

   _____

4. Sam's mom bought some soap, didn't she?

   _____

5. Sam's mom bought some cereal, didn't she?

   _____

6. Sam's dad bought some soda, didn't he?

   _____

7. Sam's mom bought some soup, didn't she?

   _____

8. Sam's mom bought some paper towels, didn't she?

   _____

9. Sam's dad bought some jam, didn't he?

   _____

10. Sam's mom bought some milk, didn't she?

    _____

11. Sam's dad bought some eggs, didn't he?

    _____

12. Sam's dad bought some cheese, didn't he?

    _____

3 B **Listen and answer.**

VOCABULARY FOCUS

He will give you some stamps if you give him money.	=	He will **sell** you some stamps.

4 A Read and answer.

1. They sell stamps at a post office. _____*True*_____
2. They sell hammers at a jewelry store. _____
3. They sell bread at a bakery. _____
4. They sell clothes at a drugstore. _____
5. They sell rings and bracelets at a jewelry store. _____
6. They sell tools at a hardware store. _____
7. They sell dishes and pans at a post office. _____
8. They sell hamburgers and French fries at a library. _____
9. They sell soap and shampoo at a drugstore. _____
10. They sell ladders at a hardware store. _____

4 B Listen and answer.

GRAMMAR FOCUS

Present	Past
sell	sold

5 Write. Use these words.

books   clubs   flowers   ladders   pans   pictures   rackets   tools

1. The construction workers needed money, _*so they sold their tools.*_
2. The chefs needed money, _____
3. The house painters needed money, _____
4. The gardeners needed money, _____
5. The artists needed money, _____
6. The golfers needed money, _____
7. The writers needed money, _____
8. The tennis players needed money, _____

present perfect

1 **Listen.**

A._____

B._____

C._____

D._____

E._____

F._____

G._____

H._____

I._____

J._____

K._____

L._____

1 **Listen and write the letters.**

1. ____
2. ____
3. ____
4. ____

5. ____
6. ____
7. ____
8. ____

9. ____
10. ____
11. ____
12. ____

Read and answer.

1. She has brushed her teeth. _____ *C*
2. She is washing the car. _____
3. She is going to plant the flowers, but she hasn't planted them yet. _____
4. She has opened the gift. _____
5. She is going to brush her teeth, but she hasn't brushed them yet. _____
6. She has washed the car. _____
7. She is brushing her teeth. _____
8. She has planted the flowers. _____
9. She is going to open the gift, but she hasn't opened it yet. _____
10. She is planting the flowers. _____
11. She is going to wash the car, but she hasn't washed it yet. _____
12. She is opening the gift. _____

2   **Look at the pictures and write answers.**

1. Is she going to open the gift?
   No, she has already opened it.

2. Is she going to brush her teeth?
   Yes, but she hasn't brushed them yet.

3. Is she going to wash the car?
   _____

4. Is she going to plant the flowers?
   _____

5. Is she going to open the gift?
   _____

6. Is she going to brush her teeth?
   _____

The tennis racket **needs repair**.

3 Write. Use these words.

bake any cakes	clean the rug	cook any rice	listen to any music
phone anyone	play any music	play any tennis	
receive any e-mails	watch any TV	weigh their baby	

1. The television needs repair.
   That's why they haven't watched any TV for three weeks.

2. The vacuum cleaner needs repair.
   _____

3. The oven needs repair.
   _____

4. The tennis racket needs repair.
   _____

5. The scale needs repair.
   _____

6. The cell phone needs repair.
   _____

7. The radio needs repair.
   _____

8. The stove needs repair.
   _____

9. The guitar needs repair.
   _____

10. The computer needs repair.
    _____

GRAMMAR FOCUS

| He took my book and he kept it. | = | He took my book and he didn't give it back. |

4 A Write. Use these words.

book	brushes	cell phone	hose	keys	matches
pans	razor	stamps	towels	vacuum cleaner	

1. Why hasn't Bill painted the house?

   Somebody took his brushes and didn't give them back.

2. Why hasn't he cleaned the rug?

   Somebody took his vacuum cleaner and didn't give it back.

3. Why hasn't he shaved?

   _____

4. Why hasn't he locked the doors?

   _____

5. Why hasn't he watered the flowers?

   _____

6. Why hasn't he cooked the rice?

   _____

7. Why hasn't he mailed the letters?

   _____

8. Why hasn't he dried his hands?

   _____

9. Why hasn't he telephoned his wife?

   _____

10. Why hasn't he started the fire?

    _____

11. Why hasn't he studied math?

    _____

4 B Listen and answer.

indirect objects
was going to

GRAMMAR FOCUS				
I gave a book to Keiko.	=	I gave Keiko a book.	=	I gave **her** a book.

1 **Write. Use these words.**

brooms	flowers	food	maps	medicine
music	paper and pencils	pictures	tools	wrenches

1. What did the mechanics give to the girl?

   They gave her some wrenches.

2. What did the artists give to the men and women?

   _____

3. What did the composers give to the people?

   _____

4. What did the teachers give to you and John?

   _____

5. What did the gardeners give to the children?

   _____

6. What did the custodians give to the students?

   _____

7. What did the waiters give to you?

   _____

8. What did the geography teachers give to their students?

   _____

9. What did the doctors give to the old man?

   _____

10. What did the constructions workers give to me?

    _____

Teacher:	Juan, what did Maria give you?
Juan:	She gave **me** a pen.
Teacher:	Paul, what did Maria give Juan?
Paul:	She gave **him** a pen.

2 **Write sentences.**

1. Bill gave his children some money.

   They have the money that Bill gave them.

2. Tom gave his sister some books.

   _____

3. The mechanic gave Rosa some wrenches.

   _____

4. The doctor gave my niece some medicine.

   _____

5. Aunt Grace gave Louis some pictures.

   _____

6. The teacher gave the boys some pencils.

   _____

7. The custodian gave Mark some brooms.

   _____

8. My mother gave me some new shoes.

   _____

9. The gardener gave my brother and me some flowers.

   _____

10. The photographer gave my cousins some photographs.

   _____

We know an old man who a house in the mountains 100 miles any city. He doesn't have electricity. He has used a microwave, he has never used a, and he have any electrical tools. He cooks all his food over a, and he reads every book he buy or borrow.

We went to visit last summer because I wanted to a story about him for our school newspaper. His house was and clean, and he didn't have a lot of, just a bed, a dresser, some chairs, and a table. He had a cow and chickens and a vegetable garden.

He told that he drove every month to a small town where there was a small library. I see books on the chairs, books on the table, and books on the floor. There were books everywhere. Most of the books library books, but some of them were books that he bought when he to town. I asked him how many books he read each month and he smiled. He said that he didn't, but that he was reading all the books in the small town's library for the time.

3 B — Write these words above the carets.

can	computer	could	doesn't	fire	from
furniture	has	him	know	me	never
second	small	some	went	were	write

3 C — Read and answer.

1. The old man has a house in the mountains. _____ *True* _____

2. He has never used a computer or a microwave. _____

3. He borrows books, but he doesn't buy any books. _____

4. His house is small, and he doesn't have a sofa. _____

5. He doesn't have any animals. _____

6. He told them that he drove to the small town to borrow books from the library. _____

7. Most of the books in his house were library books. _____

8. All of the books were on the table or on the floor. _____

9. He told them that he read 30 books every month. _____

10. He was reading all the books in the small town's library
for the second time. _____

3 **Listen and answer.**

4 **Class Activity.**

Stand next to a classmate. Ask and answer questions.

Teacher: Who is standing next to Juan?
Student: Maria is.

Sit down. Ask and answer questions.

Teacher: Who was standing next to Juan?
Student: Maria was.

Change seats. Ask and answer questions.

Teacher: Who is sitting in Maria's seat?
Student: Paul is.

4 **Return to your seat. With a partner, write sentences.**

Paul was sitting in Maria's seat.
Juan was sitting in Paul's seat.

Write sentences. Use these words.

a helmet	a hose	a radio	a spade
a vacuum cleaner	a broom	any bread	any matches
any needles	any pans	any soap	any spoons

1. Why didn't you wash your hands?

    I was going to wash them, but I didn't have any soap.

2. Why didn't you light the fire?

    _____

3. Why didn't you make the sandwich?

    _____

4. Why didn't you sweep the floor?

    _____

5. Why didn't you water the flowers?

    _____

6. Why didn't you clean the rug?

    _____

7. Why didn't you cook the rice?

    _____

8. Why didn't you sew your clothes?

    _____

9. Why didn't you plant the tree?

    _____

10. Why didn't you ride your motorcycle?

    _____

11. Why didn't you eat the soup?

    _____

12. Why didn't you listen to the music?

    _____

6 Find these words. Circle.

LITER	ROLL	BAR	POUND
GALLON	HEAD	BAG	CAN
BOTTLE	LOAF	JAR	DOZEN
QUART			

```
D  O  U  X  L  S  V  B  A  G  P  P  Z  L  Q
J  Y  I  M  P  C  C  D  N  C  Q  U  A  R  T
Q  W  T  X  P  C  F  R  A  A  D  G  A  O  T
B  G  E  F  D  O  Z  E  N  C  C  R  R  C  G
R  O  K  L  U  S  N  F  P  C  T  D  F  G  A
N  J  T  H  F  N  T  U  O  V  O  I  L  B  L
C  V  E  T  E  P  U  X  E  I  X  A  I  H  L
A  F  I  O  L  G  H  E  A  D  U  J  T  Q  O
N  O  V  G  A  E  D  M  T  R  Q  V  E  Z  N
H  D  L  G  V  X  I  J  B  T  O  W  R  P  B
E  L  C  P  L  L  O  A  F  E  H  L  F  B  K
M  O  N  W  O  T  A  O  H  L  L  P  L  O  V
S  N  G  J  B  U  N  N  L  J  S  U  H  X  A
N  N  Y  V  M  M  N  O  Z  N  L  B  E  I  Y
J  A  R  H  O  E  R  D  M  R  P  B  A  R  P
```

6 With a partner, write the words you found in alphabetical order.

bag _____   _____

_____   _____

_____   _____

_____   _____

_____   _____

_____

12 Summary

1 A Write these words on the correct lines.

found	drove	saw	ate	spoke
bought	took	sat	drank	stood

VERBS

Present	Past
buy	*bought*
drink	_____
drive	_____
eat	_____
find	_____
see	_____
sit	_____
speak	_____
stand	_____
take	_____

1 B Write. Use the past tense verbs of 1 A.

1. She _____*found*_____ her keys in her purse.
2. We _____ the movie last night.
3. They _____ the car to the library.
4. She _____ on the chair next to the window.
5. I _____ Spanish to my grandparents.
6. She _____ a new car with the money.
7. We _____ all the cereal.
8. He _____ under the umbrella.
9. You _____ all the milk.
10. They _____ the books from the teacher.

1 C Write. Use these words.

couldn't	didn't	had	was	were	weren't

1. They _____were_____ washing the dishes in hot water.
2. We _____ know how to play the guitar.
3. She _____ planting flowers when it started to rain.
4. There _____ any vegetables in the refrigerator.
5. They _____ open the door without a key.
6. She _____ to write with a pencil because she didn't have a pen.

2 Write sentences using the words.

1. cooks / he / kitchen / in / the

   He cooks in the kitchen.

2. library / in / we / the / read

   _____

3. letter / him / she / a / wrote

   _____

4. Sam / faster / they / than / run

   _____

5. crossed / desert / largest / in / the / Africa / we

   _____

6. him / can't / with / he / play

   _____

7. money / she / any / gave / never / her / to

   _____

8. their / should / clothes / wash / they / dirty

   _____

Write these words on the correct lines.

armchair	computer	hair dryer	map	razor	stove
bath towels	credit cards	hose	meat	rug	television
belts	desk	ice cream	microwave	sandals	toaster
bicycle	dictionary	jackets	milk	shampoo	tools
board	dish towels	ladder	money	soap	toothbrushes
boots	dishes	lamp	pans	soda	wallet
car	dresses	lettuce	pants	sofa	
cheese	globe	library card	pen	spade	

PURSE

pen
_____
_____
_____
_____

LIVING ROOM

television
_____
_____
_____
_____

**REFRIGERATOR/
FREEZER**

milk
_____
_____
_____
_____
_____

KITCHEN

dish towels
_____
_____
_____
_____
_____

BATHROOM

bath towels
_____
_____
_____
_____

CLOSET

jackets
_____
_____
_____
_____

WHERE?

CLASSROOM

computer
_____
_____
_____
_____
_____

GARAGE

car
_____
_____
_____
_____
_____

4 Finish each sentence. Use these words.

tomorrow	yesterday	yet

1. She painted a picture _yesterday._
   She is going to paint a picture _tomorrow._
   She hasn't painted a picture _yet._

next week	today	last week

2. She is driving her new car _____
   She will drive her new car _____
   She was going to drive her new car _____

every day	tomorrow	yesterday

3. They eat all the vegetables _____
   They ate all the vegetables _____
   They are going to eat all the vegetables _____

tomorrow night	every night	last night

4. He will see the stars _____
   He can see the stars _____
   He could see the stars _____

often	yet	before we ate

5. We should wash our hands _____
   We had to wash our hands _____
   We haven't washed our hands _____

after she arrived	but we didn't	every day

6. We must study _____
   We didn't study _____
   We were going to study _____

5   **Write sentences. Use *who, where,* or *that.***

1. The man is sleeping. We can see the man.

   We can see the man who is sleeping.

2. He is eating in the room. We can see the room.

   We can see the room where he is eating.

3. The fire is burning. We can see the fire.

   We can see the fire that is burning.

4. She is reading a book. We bought the book.

   _____

5. The woman is driving the truck. We know the woman.

   _____

6. They keep their car in the garage. We painted the garage.

   _____

7. The children are learning English. She is teaching the children.

   _____

8. The hammer was in the tool box. We used the hammer.

   _____

9. His sister teaches English at a big school. They go to the big school.

   _____

10. He cooked the rice. We are eating the rice.

    _____

11. The children gave us flowers. We kissed the children.

    _____

12. She keeps her rings in a jewelry box. She can't find the jewelry box.

    _____

Back of the Book

Chapter 1

LESSON 1

PAGE 2 **1. A.** Read the following three times. Say the letter each time; for example: A (pause), colors B (pause) family members.

A. colors	E. days of the week	I. consonants
B. family members	F. nationalities	J. opposites
C. parts of the body	G. places	K. quantities
D. sports	H. vowels	L. clothes

PAGE 3 **1. B.** Read the following. The students write the corresponding letters on the lines provided.

1. clothes
2. days of the week
3. parts of the body
4. colors and sports
5. consonants and vowels
6. opposites and nationalities
7. colors, places, and clothes
8. quantities, nationalities, and sports
9. family members, vowels, and opposites
10. days of the week, quantities, and consonants
11. places, family members, and parts of the body
12. vowels, consonants, and days of the week

PAGE 3 **1. C.** Spell each word. The students write the words on the lines provided.

A. colors C O L O R S colors
B. family members family F A M I L Y members M E M B E R S family members
C. parts of the body parts P A R T S of O F the T H E body B O D Y parts of the body
D. sports S P O R T S sports
E. days of the week days D A Y S of O F the T H E week W E E K days of the week
F. nationalities N A T I O N A L I T I E S nationalities
G. places P L A C E S places
H. vowels V O W E L S vowels
I. consonants C O N S O N A N T S consonants
J. opposites O P P O S I T E S opposites
K. quantities Q U A N T I T I E S quantities
L. clothes C L O T H E S clothes

PAGE 3 **2. B.** Read the sentences of 2. A. The students write TRUE or FALSE on a sheet of paper.

LESSON 2

PAGE 6 **1. A.** Say the alphabet. Say the alphabet again, pausing after each letter for the students to repeat.

PAGE 7 **1. C.** Read the questions of 1. B. The students write YES or NO on a sheet of paper.

PAGE 8 **3. A.** Read the following three times. Say the letter each time; for example: A (pause) return address, B (pause) first name.

A. return address	D. last name	G. city
B. first name	E. street address	H. state
C. middle initial	F. apartment number	I. Zip Code

PAGE 8 **3. B.** Read the following. The students write the corresponding letters on the lines provided.

1. last name
2. city
3. apartment number
4. state and zip code
5. street address and return address
6. middle initial and first name
7. street address, apartment number, and city
8. zip code, state, and city
9. last name, first name, and middle initial

PAGE 8 **3. C.** Spell each word. The students write the words on the lines provided.

A. return address return R E T U R N address A D D R E S S return address
B. first name first F I R S T name N A M E first name
C. middle initial middle M I D D L E initial I N I T I A L middle initial

D. last name last L A S T name N A M E last name
E. street address street S T R E E T address A D D R E S S street address
F. apartment number apartment A P A R T M E N T number N U M B E R apartment number
G. city C I T Y city
H. state S T A T E state
I. zip code zip Z I P code C O D E code

LESSON 3

`PAGE 10` **1. B.** Read the questions of 1. A. The students write YES or NO on a sheet of paper.

`PAGE 12` **3. B.** Read the questions of 3. A. The students write the opposite or "It doesn't have an opposite." on a sheet of paper.

`PAGE 12` **4. A.** Read the following dialog. Some words are in italics; these words are missing in the student section. Tell the students that there are fifteen words missing but that there are no spaces where those words are missing. Instruct the students to put a caret (ʌ) wherever there is a word missing. (The first caret has been placed for the students.) Read the dialog at least three times.

Allison:	Dad, what is the capital city *of* California?
Dad:	I *don't* know. Ask your mother.
Allison:	Mom, what's *the* capital of California?
Mom:	I don't know. Ask your grandmother. *She'll* know.
Allison:	Grandma, *do* you know California's capital city?
Grandmother:	*It's* Sacramento.
Allison:	Is Sacramento *two* words?
Grandmother:	No, it's just *one* word.
Allison:	Are there two *e*'s *in* Sacramento?
Grandmother:	No, just one *e* but it *has* two *a*'s.
Allison:	*Is* it capital S-a-c-r-a-m-e-n-t-o?
Grandmother:	Yes, that's right. It's *a* Spanish word. There *are* a lot *of* cities in California that *have* Spanish names.

`PAGE 13` **4. B.** After the students have put in all the carets in 4. A., instruct them to write the missing words above each caret.

Chapter 2

LESSON 1

`PAGE 14` **1. A.** Read the following three times. Say the letter each time; for example: A (pause) book bag, B (pause) bookcase.

A. book bag	D. clock	G. board	J. globe	M. notebook
B. bookcase	E. window	H. wall	K. keyboard	N. floor
C. dictionary	F. wastebasket	I. door	L. table	

`PAGE 14` **1. B.** Read the following. The students write the corresponding letters on the lines provided.

1. clock
2. bookcase
3. window
4. table and wastebasket
5. wall and board
6. notebook and keyboard
7. globe and book bag
8. dictionary and bookcase
9. window, door, and floor
10. dictionary, notebook, and book bag
11. keyboard, globe, and clock
12. wastebasket, board, and table

`PAGE 15` **1. C.** Spell each word. The students write the words on the lines provided.

A. book bag book B O O K bag B A G book bag
B. bookcase B O O K C A S E bookcase
C. dictionary D I C T I O N A R Y dictionary
D. clock C L O C K clock
E. window W I N D O W window
F. wastebasket W A S T E B A S K E T wastebasket
G. board B O A R D board
H. wall W A L L wall
I. door D O O R door
J. globe G L O B E globe
K. keyboard K E Y B O A R D keyboard
L. table T A B L E table
M. notebook N O T E B O O K notebook
N. floor F L O O R floor

`PAGE 15` **2. B.** Read the sentences of 2. A. The students write TRUE of FALSE on a sheet of paper.

LESSON 2

PAGE 18 **1. A.** Read the following school subjects three times. Say the letter each time; for example: A (pause) math, B (pause) English.

A. math
B. English
C. health
D. history
E. geography
F. biology
G. computer science
H. art
I. physical education

PAGE 19 **1. B.** Read the following. The students write the corresponding letters on the lines provided.

1. English
2. math
3. art
4. history and geography
5. biology and health
6. computer science and physical education
7. art and math
8. physical education and health
9. English and history
10. computer science, geography, and biology

PAGE 19 **1. C.** Spell each word. The students write the words on the lines provided.

A. math M A T H math
B. English E N G L I S H English
C. health H E A L T H health
D. history H I S T O R Y history
E. geography G E O G R A P H Y geography
F. biology B I O L O G Y biology
G. computer science computer C O M P U T E R science S C I E N C E computer science
H. art A R T art
I. physical education physical P H Y S I C A L education E D U C A T I O N physical education

PAGE 19 **2. B.** Read the questions of 2. A. The students write the answers on a sheet of paper.

PAGE 20 **3. A.** Read the following class schedules.

Class Schedule for Keiko Yamaguchi.
History in room 310 on Mondays, Wednesdays, and Fridays at 9:00.
Math in room 202 on Mondays, Wednesdays, and Fridays at 11:00.
Art in room 105 on Thursdays at 2:00.
English in room 212 on Mondays, Tuesdays, Wednesdays, and Fridays at 3:00.
Health in room 314 on Wednesdays at 5:00.
Computer science in room 340 on Tuesdays and Thursdays at 5:00.

Class Schedule for Miguel Santos.
History in room 310 on Mondays, Wednesdays, and Fridays at 9:00.
Biology in room 223 on Mondays, Wednesdays, and Fridays at 1:00.
Art in room 105 on Thursdays at 2:00.
English in room 212 on Mondays, Tuesdays, Wednesdays, and Fridays at 3:00.
Math in room 151 on Tuesdays and Thursdays at 4:30.
Geography in room 235 on Tuesdays and Thursdays at 7:00.

PAGE 22 **5. A.** Read the following dialog. Tell the students that there are sixteen words missing and instruct them to put a caret (ʌ) wherever there is a word missing.

Marlena: Can you tell *me* where the art room is?
Rita: Sure, what's *its* number?
Marlena: Let's see. It's *room* 105.
Rita: Oh, that's *next* to the gym. Do you *know* where that is?
Marlena: I don't know where any *of* the rooms are.
Rita: What hour is *your* art class?
Marlena: It's *at* 10:00.
Rita: Hey, we have the *same* class. Let's see, it's 8:55 now. What class *do* you have at 9:00?
Marlena: History. It's *in* room 210.
Rita: Great, we have the same history *class* too. After history class, we *can* go to art class together.
Marlena: When do you have lunch?
Rita: At 11:00.
Marlena: Me too. Can we *eat* lunch together? I don't know anybody.
Rita: Sure. I eat lunch *with* Maria, Juan, and Sara. We can *all* have lunch together.

LESSON 3

PAGE 25 **2. A.** Read the following three times. Say the letter each time; for example: A (pause) T-shirt, B (pause) socks.

A. T-shirt
B. socks
C. boots

D. coat
E. sweater
F. shorts

G. cap
H. hat
I. jeans

PAGE 25 **2. B.** Read the following. The students write the corresponding letters on the lines provided.

1. coat
2. hat
3. T-shirt

4. boots and socks
5. jeans and shorts
6. sweater and coat

7. hat, cap, and T-shirt
8. jeans, sweater, and socks
9. boots, shorts, and cap

PAGE 25 **2. C.** Spell each word. The students write the words on the lines provided.

A. T-shirt T - S H I R T T-shirt
B. socks S O C K S socks
C. boots B O O T S boots

D. coat C O A T coat
E. sweater S W E A T E R sweater
F. shorts S H O R T S shorts

G. cap C A P cap
H. hat H A T hat
I. jeans J E A N S jeans

PAGE 25 **3. A.** Read the following sentences, pointing to the Roman numerals in the pictures A-D.

A. This is a Roman numeral.
B. That is a Roman numeral.

C. These are Roman numerals.
D. Those are Roman numerals.

Chapter 3

LESSON 1

PAGE 28 **1. A.** Read the following three times.

A. the earth
B. the earth turns
C. the sun
D. the sun rises
E. the sun shines

F. the sun sets
G. flowers
H. flowers grow
I. the planets
J. the planets circle the sun

PAGE 29 **1. B.** Read the following. The students write the corresponding letters on the lines provided.

1. the planets
2. the earth
3. flowers
4. the sun rises and the sun sets
5. the sun shines and flowers grow

6. the earth and the earth turns
7. the sun rises and flowers grow
8. the planets, the planets circle the sun, and the earth turns
9. the sun rises, the sun shines, and the sun sets

PAGE 29 **1. C.** Spell each word. The students write the words on the lines provided.

A. the earth E A R T H the earth
B. the earth turns turns T U R N S the earth turns
C. the sun S U N the sun
D. the sun rises rises R I S E S the sun rises
E. the sun shines shines S H I N E S the sun shines
F. the sun sets sets S E T S the sun sets
G. flowers F L O W E R S flowers
H. flowers grow grow G R O W flowers grow
I. the planets P L A N E T S the planets
J. the planets circle the sun circle C I R C L E the planets circle the sun

PAGE 29 **2. B.** Read the questions of 2. A. The students write YES or NO on a sheet of paper.

PAGE 30 **3. A.** Read the following three times.

A. rubber bands
B. wood
C. ice
D. tomatoes

E. butterflies
F. trees
G. bounce
H. climb

I. melt
J. stretch
K. freeze
L. burn

3. B. Read the following. The students write the corresponding letters on the lines provided.

1. trees
2. wood
3. butterflies
4. ice and tomatoes
5. rubber bands and stretch

6. ice and freeze
7. trees and climb
8. wood, burn, and melt
9. bounce, stretch, and burn
10. melt, freeze, and climb

3. C. Spell each word. The students write the words on the lines provided.

A. rubber bands rubber R U B B E R bands B A N D S rubber bands
B. wood W O O D wood
C. ice I C E ice
D. tomatoes T O M A T O E S tomatoes
E. butterflies B U T T E R F L I E S butterflies
F. trees T R E E S trees
G. bounce B O U N C E bounce
H. climb C L I M B climb
I. melt M E L T melt
J. stretch S T R E T C H stretch
K. freeze F R E E Z E freeze
L. burn B U R N burn

4. B. Read the questions of 4. A. The students write YES or NO on a sheet of paper.

LESSON 2

1. A. Read the following three times.

A. morning
B. noon
C. afternoon
D. evening
E. night

F. midnight
G. breakfast
H. lunch
I. dinner
J. snack

1. B. Read the following. The students write the corresponding letters on the lines provided.

1. noon
2. night
3. lunch

4. morning and breakfast
5. noon and lunch
6. evening and dinner

7. afternoon, night, and snack
8. midnight, morning, and afternoon
9. evening, midnight, and breakfast

1. C. Spell each word. The students write the words on the lines provided.

A. morning M O R N I N G morning
B. noon N O O N noon
C. afternoon A F T E R N O O N afternoon
D. evening E V E N I N G evening
E. night N I G H T night

F. midnight M I D N I G H T midnight
G. breakfast B R E A K F A S T breakfast
H. lunch L U N C H lunch
I. dinner D I N N E R dinner
J. snack S N A C K snack

3. B. Read the questions of 3. A. The students write YES or NO on a sheet of paper.

LESSON 3

1. A. Read the following three times.

A. carrots
B. peas
C. corn

D. rice
E. cereal
F. chicken

G. beef
H. chocolate
I. sandwich

J. soup
K. hamburger
L. French fries

1. B. Read the following. The students write the corresponding letters on the lines provided.

1. chocolate
2. corn
3. carrots

4. soup and sandwich
5. hamburger and French fries
6. chicken and rice

7. beef, peas, and chicken
8. cereal, corn, and rice
9. carrots, peas, and soup

PAGE 37 **1. C.** Spell each word. The students write the words on the lines provided.

A. carrots C A R R O T S carrots
B. peas P E A S peas
C. corn C O R N corn
D. rice R I C E rice
E. cereal C E R E A L cereal
F. chicken C H I C K E N chicken

G. beef B E E F beef
H. chocolate C H O C O L A T E chocolate
I. sandwich S A N D W I C H sandwich
J. soup S O U P soup
K. hamburger H A M B U R G E R hamburger
L. French fries French F R E N C H fries F R I E S French fries

PAGE 37 **2. B.** Read the sentences of 2. A. The students write TRUE or FALSE on a sheet of paper.

PAGE 38 **3. B.** Read the questions of 3. A. The students write YES or NO on a sheet of paper.

LESSON 4

PAGE 40 **1. A.** Read the following three times.

A. buy
B. catch
C. lock

D. kill
E. money
F. mousetrap

G. key
H. bug spray
I. knife

J. match
K. driver's license
L. shampoo

PAGE 40 **1. B.** Read the following. The students write the corresponding letters on the lines provided.

1. money
2. key
3. knife
4. bug spray and shampoo
5. mousetrap and knife
6. match and driver's license

7. lock and catch
8. kill and buy
9. key, lock, and match
10. bug spray, kill, and buy
11. catch, mousetrap, and money
12. driver's license, money, and shampoo

PAGE 41 **1. C.** Spell each word. The students write the words on the lines provided.

A. buy B U Y buy
B. catch C A T C H catch
C. lock L O C K lock
D. kill K I L L kill
E. money M O N E Y money
F. mousetrap M O U S E T R A P mousetrap
G. key K E Y key
H. bug spray bug B U G spray S P R A Y bug spray
I. knife K N I F E knife
J. match M A T C H match
K. driver's license driver's D R I V E R ' S license L I C E N S E driver's license
L. shampoo S H A M P O O shampoo

PAGE 42 **4. A.** Read the following dialog. Tell the students that there are twenty words missing and instruct them to put a caret (∧) wherever there is a word missing.

Bob: Hi, Jim. Is it true that you have a *new* baby sister?
Jim: It sure is. *Her* name is Peggy Ann.
Bob: I *like* that name. Aren't those your *aunts'* names?
Jim: That's right. I *have* an Aunt Peggy and an Aunt Ann.
Bob: How much *does* Peggy Ann weigh?
Jim: 12 1/2 pounds. She *eats* all the time.
Bob: Well, that's what babies *do*. They eat and *sleep*.
Jim: Yes, and they *cry*.
Bob: *Does* she cry a lot?
Jim: She doesn't cry in the day, but *every* night at midnight she *cries*. My father and mother hold her and then *she* stops. But every time they *put* her in bed she cries.
Bob: So *what* do they do?
Jim: Well, they *play* with her and they sing to her, but she *doesn't* stop.
Bob: Are *your* parents tired?
Jim: Yes, they're exhausted! They don't go to bed *before* the sun rises.

Chapter 4

LESSON 1

`PAGE 44` 1. A. Read the following three times.

A. hammer
B. nails
C. saw
D. wrench
E. nuts and bolts
F. screwdriver
G. screws
H. pliers
I. tape measure
J. drill
K. circular saw
L. flashlight

`PAGE 45` 1. B. Read the following. The students write the corresponding letters on the lines provided.

1. screwdriver
2. saw
3. hammer
4. tape measure
5. pliers and circular saw
6. nuts and bolts and screws
7. wrench and nuts and bolts
8. drill and flashlight
9. saw, nails, and hammer
10. screwdriver, screws, and drill
11. wrench, nuts and bolts, and pliers
12. tape measure, flashlight, and circular saw

`PAGE 45` 1. C. Spell each word. The students write the words on the lines provided.

A. hammer H A M M E R hammer
B. nails N A I L S nails
C. saw S A W saw
D. wrench W R E N C H wrench
E. nuts and bolts nuts N U T S and A N D bolts B O L T S nuts and bolts
F. screwdriver S C R E W D R I V E R screwdriver
G. screws S C R E W S screws
H. pliers P L I E R S pliers
I. tape measure tape T A P E measure M E A S U R E tape measure
J. drill D R I L L drill
K. circular saw circular C I R C U L A R saw S A W circular saw
L. flashlight F L A S H L I G H T flashlight

`PAGE 46` 3. A. Read the following three times.

A. raincoat
B. apron
C. earphones
D. swimsuit
E. pajamas
F. sweat suit
G. helmet
H. safety glasses

`PAGE 46` 3. B. Read the following. The students write the corresponding letters on the lines provided.

1. pajamas
2. apron
3. helmet
4. raincoat and swimsuit
5. earphones and pajamas
6. sweat suit and swimsuit
7. raincoat, helmet, and safety glasses
8. apron, pajamas, and sweat suit
9. earphones, safety glasses, and helmet

`PAGE 46` 3. C. Spell each word. The students write the words on the lines provided.

A. raincoat R A I N C O A T raincoat
B. apron A P R O N apron
C. earphones E A R P H O N E S earphones
D. swimsuit S W I M S U I T swimsuit
E. pajamas P A J A M A S pajamas
F. sweat suit sweat S W E A T suit S U I T sweat suit
G. helmet H E L M E T helmet
H. safety glasses safety S A F E T Y glasses G L A S S E S safety glasses

`PAGE 47` 5. B. Read the questions of 5. A. The students write YES or NO on a sheet of paper.

LESSON 2

`PAGE 48` 1. A. Read the following three times.

A. custodian. The custodian is sweeping the floor. custodian
B. construction workers. The construction workers are hammering and sawing. construction workers
C. pilot. The pilot is flying an airplane. pilot
D. painters. The painters are painting a house. painters
E. mechanic. The mechanic is repairing a car. mechanic
F. photographer. The photographer is taking photographs. photographer
G. chefs. The chefs are cooking food. chefs

H. waiters. The waiters are serving food. waiters
I. beautician. The beautician is cutting hair. beautician
J. gardeners. The gardeners are planting a tree. gardeners

PAGE 48 **1. B.** Read the following. The students write the corresponding letters on the lines provided.

1. painters
2. pilot
3. waiters
4. mechanic
5. custodian and chefs
6. construction workers and photographer
7. gardeners and beautician
8. photographer, custodian, and mechanic
9. waiters, chefs, and pilot
10. beautician, construction workers, and gardeners

PAGE 49 **1 .C.** Spell each word. The students write the words on the lines provided.

A. custodian C U S T O D I A N custodian
B. construction workers construction C O N S T R U C T I O N workers W O R K E R S construction workers
C. pilot P I L O T pilot
D. painters P A I N T E R S painters
E. mechanic M E C H A N I C mechanic
F. photographer P H O T O G R A P H E R photographer
G. chefs C H E F S chefs
H. waiters W A I T E R S waiters
I. beautician B E A U T I C I A N beautician
J. gardeners G A R D E N E R S gardeners

LESSON 3

PAGE 52 **1. A.** Read the following three times.

A. leave
B. arrive
C. start
D. finish
E. get in
F. get out
G. turn on
H. turn off
I. drop
J. float
K. heat
L. break

PAGE 52 **1. B.** Read the following. The students write the corresponding letters on the lines provided.

1. heat
2. break
3. drop
4. leave
5. turn on
6. float
7. start and finish
8. get in and get out
9. arrive and leave
10. turn on, turn off, and get out
11. drop, float, and break
12. heat, turn off, and finish

PAGE 52 **1. C.** Spell each word. The students write the words on the lines provided.

A. leave L E A V E leave
B. arrive A R R I V E arrive
C. start S T A R T start
D. finish F I N I S H finish
E. get in get G E T in I N get in
F. get out get G E T out O U T get out
G. turn on turn T U R N on O N turn on
H. turn off turn T U R N off O F F turn off
I. drop D R O P drop
J. float F L O A T float
K. heat H E A T heat
L. break B R E A K break

PAGE 54 **3. B.** Read the questions of 3. A. The students write YES or NO on a sheet of paper.

PAGE 56 **6. A.** Read the following dialog. Tell the students that there are eighteen words missing and instruct them to put a caret (∧) wherever there is a word missing.

Girl: Mama, *is* it 6:00?
Mama: No, *not* yet. It's 5:45.
Girl: Mama, is *it* 6:00?
Mama: No, not yet. *It's* 5:50.
Girl: Mama, is it *6:00*?
Mama: No, not *yet*. It's 5:57.
Girl: Mama, is it 6:00 yet?
Mama: Yes, now *it's* 6:00.
Girl: *Can* we go in now?
Mama: Yes, now we can *go* in.
Girl: What time is the movie going *to* start?
Mama: *At* 6:30.
Girl: Can I *have* some popcorn and a soda before it starts?
Mama: Yes.
Girl: Can I have a big box *of* popcorn and a big soda?

Mama: No, that's *too* much.

Girl: *Can* I have some chocolate candy?

Mama: No, it isn't good *to* eat too much.

Girl: Mama?

Mama: Yes?

Girl: Is it *6:30* yet?

Mama: No, not yet. It's *6:10*.

Chapter 5

LESSON 1

PAGE 58 **1. A.** Read the following three times.

A. presidents, Abraham Lincoln and Sun Yat-sen, presidents

B. writers, William Shakespeare and Jane Austen, writers

C. artists, Pablo Picasso and Leonardo da Vinci, artists

D. composers, Ludwig von Beethoven and Giacomo Puccini, composers

E. scientists, Albert Einstein and Marie Curie, scientists

F. astronauts, Neil Armstrong and Yuri Gagarin, astronauts

PAGE 58 **1. B.** Read the following. The students write the corresponding letters on the lines provided.

1. artists
2. presidents
3. astronauts
4. composers and writers
5. scientists and astronauts
6. presidents and composers
7. writers and artists
8. presidents, writers, and composers
9. astronauts, scientists, and artists

PAGE 59 **1. C.** Spell each word. The students write the words on the lines provided.

A. presidents P R E S I D E N T S presidents

B. writers W R I T E R S writers

C. artists A R T I S T S artists

D. composers C O M P O S E R S composers

E. scientists S C I E N T I S T S scientists

F. astronauts A S T R O N A U T S astronauts

PAGE 59 **2. B.** Read the questions of 2. A. The students write YES or NO on a sheet of paper.

PAGE 60 **3. A.** Read the following. The students write the dates on the lines provided.

1. Beethoven was born in 1770 and died in 1827.
2. Shakespeare was born in 1564 and died in 1616.
3. Lincoln was born in 1809 and died in 1865.
4. Sun Yat-sen was born in 1866 and died in 1925.
5. Marie Curie was born in 1867 and died in 1934.
6. Puccini was born in 1858 and died in 1924.
7. Leonardo da Vinci was born in 1452 and died in 1519.
8. Yuri Gagarin was born in 1934 and died in 1968.
9. Jane Austen was born in 1775 and died in 1817.
10. Picasso was born in 1881 and died in 1973.
11. Einstein was born in 1879 and died in 1955.
12. Neil Armstrong was born in 1930.

LESSON 2

PAGE 62 **1. A.** Read the following three times.

A. Sophie brushed her teeth.
B. Sophie painted a picture.
C. Sophie mowed the grass.
D. Sophie dried her hair.
E. Sophie erased the board.
F. Sophie killed some insects.
G. Sophie washed her car.
H. Sophie baked a cake.
I. Sophie planted some flowers.
J. Sophie cleaned her room.
K. Sophie closed the door.
L. Sophie opened the window.

PAGE 62 **1. B.** Read the following. The students write the corresponding letters on the lines provided.

1. Sophie painted a picture.
2. Sophie washed her car.
3. Sophie brushed her teeth.
4. Sophie killed some insects.
5. Sophie baked a cake.
6. Sophie cleaned her room.
7. Sophie mowed the grass, and she planted some flowers.
8. Sophie opened the window, and she closed the door.
9. Sophie erased the board, and she dried her hair.
10. Sophie cleaned her room, she mowed the grass, and she washed her car.
11. Sophie dried her hair, she baked a cake, and she brushed her teeth.
12. Sophie opened the window, she erased the board, and she closed the door.

PAGE 63 **2. B.** Read the sentences of 2. A. The students write TRUE or FALSE on a sheet of paper.

4. A. Spell each word. The students write the words on the lines provided.

1. closed C L O S E D closed
2. cried C R I E D cried
3. erased E R A S E D erased
4. locked L O C K E D locked
5. opened O P E N E D opened

6. painted P A I N T E D painted
7. smiled S M I L E D smiled
8. touched T O U C H E D touched
9. wanted W A N T E D wanted
10. washed W A S H E D washed

LESSON 3

PAGE 66 **1. A.** Tell the students to look at the back cover. Say the following three times.

1. Brown and white make tan.
2. Red and yellow make orange.
3. Blue and yellow make green.
4. Red and blue make purple.
5. Black and blue make dark blue.
6. White and blue make light blue.

PAGE 66 **1. C.** Read the questions of 1. B. The students write "Yes, they do." or "No, they don't." on a sheet of paper.

PAGE 68 **4. A.** Read the following passage. Tell the students that there are eighteen words missing, and instruct them to put a caret (∧) wherever there is a word missing.

Our grandmother *was* born in 1899, and she died in 1998. She was almost 100 years old when she *died*. She cooked and cleaned *every* day, but she was also a very good artist. She *liked* to sit next to a big window, listen to music by Beethoven, and *paint* pictures of her family. She had *eleven* grandchildren, and she *wanted* to paint pictures of them *all*. My cousin Catherine was older *than* the other grandchildren, so she painted her *first*. Everybody was older than I was, so she painted me *last*. When she started painting *my* picture the only paints she had *were* blue, white, and black. She painted me in blue, *light* blue, and dark blue. I *like* the picture very much. I like it more than any *other* picture she ever painted. My grandmother *named* my painting "Grandma's Picasso" because Picasso painted many pictures *in* blue.

Chapter 6

PAGE 73 **4. A.** Read the following telephone conversation. Tell the students that there are twenty words missing, and instruct them to put a caret (∧) wherever there is a word missing.

Mrs. Edwards:	Hello.
Kim:	Hello, Mrs. Edwards. This *is* Kim Johnson. Is Cindy home?
Mrs. Edwards:	Just a minute, Kim. I'll call *her*.
	Cindy, *it's* Kim Johnson on the phone.
Cindy:	Hi, Kim. *Did* you study your math?
Kim:	Yes, I studied it *before* dinner. But after dinner Rob called and he *asked* me to go to the basketball game *with* him on Friday. Is it okay with you if I *don't* go with you and Sara?
Cindy:	Everybody *knows* that you like Rob. It's okay.
Kim:	*Are* you sure?
Cindy:	It's okay. We'll ask Carlos and Mark to go with *us*. We can all meet *at* the game.
Kim:	Oh, we *aren't* going to the game *at* our school. We're going *to* the game at Rob's school.
Cindy:	Well, okay, I . . .
Kim:	And I *have* one other question. Can I borrow *your* dark blue skirt?
Cindy:	But, Kim, you already have *my* light blue sweater. You borrowed that *last* week.
Kim:	Yes, I know. But I need your light blue sweater to *wear* with your dark blue skirt.

Chapter 7

LESSON 1

PAGE 74 **1. A.** Read the following three times.

A. oranges	D. butter	G. pie	J. meat
B. ham	E. juice	H. fruit	K. dairy products
C. cheese	F. ice cream	I. vegetables	L. desserts

PAGE 75 **1. B.** Read the following. The students write the corresponding letters on the lines provided.

1. fruit
2. meat
3. ice cream and pie
4. butter and cheese
5. vegetables and desserts
6. ham and oranges
7. dairy products and juice
8. ice cream, dairy products, and desserts
9. fruit, vegetables, and meat
10. juice, oranges, and ham

PAGE 75 1. C. Spell each word. The students write the words on the lines provided.

A. oranges O R A N G E S oranges
B. ham H A M ham
C. cheese C H E E S E cheese
D. butter B U T T E R butter
E. juice J U I C E juice
F. ice cream ice I C E cream C R E A M ice cream
G. pie P I E pie
H. fruit F R U I T fruit
I. vegetables V E G E T A B L E S vegetables
J. meat M E A T meat
K. dairy products dairy D A I R Y products P R O D U C T S dairy products
L. desserts D E S S E R T S desserts

PAGE 75 2. B. Read the questions of 2. A. The students write YES or NO on a sheet of paper.

PAGE 76 3. A. Put some money and several objects (some paper clips, a book, two or three pens, three or four pencils, a sheet of paper, a rubber band) on a table. Cover these objects. Uncover them and let all of the students look at the objects for ten to fifteen seconds. Then re-cover them.

PAGE 77 3. C. Read these sentences. The students write TRUE or FALSE on a sheet of paper.

1. We saw a rubber band.
2. We saw a book.
3. We saw three yellow pencils.
4. We saw two pennies.
5. We saw a sheet of paper.
6. We saw six pens.
7. We saw three dollars.
8. We saw some paper clips.
9. We saw a half sheet of paper.
10. We saw a red pen.

LESSON 2

PAGE 78 1. B. Read the questions of 1. A. The students write YES or NO on a sheet of paper.

PAGE 79 2. B. Read the sentences of 2. A. The students write TRUE or FALSE on a sheet of paper.

PAGE 80 3. B. Read the following questions. The students write answers on the lines provided.

1. Why couldn't the girl open the door?
2. Why couldn't the girl mail the letter?
3. Why couldn't the girl see the planets?
4. Why couldn't the girl burn the paper?
5. Why couldn't the girl plant the tree?
6. Why couldn't the girl drive the car?

PAGE 81 5. A. Read the following passage. Tell the students that there are eighteen words missing, and instruct them to put a caret (ᴧ) wherever there is a word missing.

Lisa's grandmother and grandfather *were* vegetarians. They *never* ate meat. When she went to their house for Sunday dinner, they *ate* rice, vegetables, cheese, fruit, salads, and eggs. For dessert they usually ate *an* apple or other fruit, but sometimes they *had* ice cream. Lisa's grandparents drank water, *milk*, and vegetable juice. They *liked* tomato juice, so they often *drank* tomato juice *before* they ate dinner. They never drank tea or coffee, and they never drank cola or any *kind* of soda. Her grandparents knew how *to* cook good meals *without* meat. Lisa *always* ate all her food at their house because *it* was so good. Today, Lisa's grandchildren come to *her* house for dinner. She cooks *them* good meals with *vegetables* and rice just like the meals she ate *at* her grandparents' house.

PAGE 81 5. D. Read the sentences of 5. C. The students write TRUE or FALSE on a sheet of paper.

LESSON 3

PAGE 82 1. A. Read the following three times.

A. students
B. library card
C. cell phone
D. umbrella
E. race
F. gift
G. study
H. win
I. lift
J. sing

B. Read the following. The students write the corresponding letters on the lines provided.

1. umbrella
2. students
3. gift
4. library card and cell phone
5. race and umbrella

6. win and lift
7. study and sing
8. students, study, and library card
9. cell phone, race, and gift
10. sing, win, and lift

C. Spell each word. The students write the words on the lines provided.

A. students S T U D E N T S students
B. library card library L I B R A R Y card C A R D library card
C. cell phone cell C E L L phone P H O N E cell phone
D. umbrella U M B R E L L A umbrella
E. race R A C E race

F. gift G I F T gift
G. study S T U D Y study
H. win W I N win
I. lift L I F T lift
J. sing S I N G sing

A. Read the following three times.

1. North America
2. South America
3. Europe
4. Africa
5. Asia

6. Australia
7. Antarctica
8. Pacific Ocean
9. Atlantic Ocean
10. Indian Ocean

11. Los Angeles
12. Toronto
13. New York
14. Mexico City
15. Bogota

16. Rio de Janeiro
17. London
18. Madrid
19. Cairo
20. Cape Town

21. Moscow
22. Beijing
23. Tokyo
24. Taipei
25. Sydney

B. Read the questions of 4. A. The students answer orally.

Chapter 8

LESSON 1

A. Read the following once.

1. Pacific Ocean
2. Mississippi River
3. Amazon River
4. Atlantic Ocean
5. Sahara Desert

6. Nile River
7. Mt. Kilimanjaro
8. Kalahari Desert
9. Africa
10. Indian Ocean

11. Gobi Desert
12. Mt. Everest
13. Asia
14. Mt. Fuji
15. Australia

Read the following, pausing after each item for students to write the size on the lines provided.

1. Pacific Ocean-sixty-four million one hundred eighty-six thousand three hundred square miles, sixty-four million one hundred eighty-six thousand three hundred
2. Mississippi River-two thousand three hundred forty miles, two thousand three hundred forty
3. Amazon River-four thousand miles, four thousand
4. Atlantic Ocean-thirty-three million four hundred twenty thousand square miles, thirty-three million four hundred twenty thousand
5. Sahara Desert-three million five hundred thousand square miles, three million five hundred thousand
6. Nile River-four thousand one hundred sixty miles, four thousand one hundred sixty
7. Mt. Kilimanjaro-nineteen thousand three hundred forty feet, nineteen thousand three hundred forty
8. Kalahari Desert-two hundred twenty-five thousand square miles, two hundred twenty-five thousand
9. Africa-eleven million seven hundred seven thousand square miles, eleven million seven hundred seven thousand
10. Indian Ocean-twenty-eight million three hundred fifty thousand five hundred square miles, twenty-eight million three hundred fifty thousand five hundred
11. Gobi Desert-five hundred thousand square miles, five hundred thousand
12. Mt. Everest-twenty-nine thousand thirty-five feet, twenty-nine thousand thirty-five
13. Asia-seventeen million one hundred twenty-nine thousand square miles, seventeen million one hundred twenty-nine thousand
14. Mt. Fuji-twelve thousand three hundred eighty-eight feet, twelve thousand three hundred eighty-eight
15. Australia-two million nine hundred sixty-six thousand square miles, two million nine hundred sixty-six thousand

A. Read the following three times.

A. river
B. desert

C. mountain
D. ocean

E. continent
F. the world

B. Read the following. The students write the corresponding letters on the lines provided.

1. ocean
2. mountain
3. continent
4. river and desert

5. the world and continent
6. mountain and river
7. ocean and continent
8. river, ocean, and the world

PAGE 90 **2. C.** Spell each word. The students write the words on the lines provided.

A. river R I V E R river
B. desert D E S E R T desert
C. mountain M O U N T A I N mountain

D. ocean O C E A N ocean
E. continent C O N T I N E N T continent
F. the world world W O R L D the world

PAGE 91 **3. B.** Read the questions of 3. A. The students answer orally.

LESSON 2

PAGE 92 **1. A.** Read the following three times.

A. rich people, rich
B. poor people, poor
C. a sick person, sick
D. a healthy person, healthy

E. heavy people, heavy
F. thin people, thin
G. a strong person, strong
H. a weak person, weak

I. a good driver, good
J. a bad driver, bad
K. a sour fruit, sour
L. a sweet fruit, sweet

M. a nice dog, nice
N. a mean dog, mean
O. a light room, light
P. a dark room, dark

PAGE 93 **1. B.** Read the following. The students write the corresponding letters on the lines provided.

1. heavy
2. sick
3. strong

4. weak and poor
5. rich and bad
6. dark and light

7. sour and mean
8. nice and good
9. thin, sweet, and sour

10. healthy, sick, and rich
11. strong, weak, and poor
12. good, bad, and nice

PAGE 93 **1. C.** Spell each word. The students write the words on the lines provided.

A. rich people rich R I C H rich people
B. poor people poor P O O R poor people
C. a sick person sick S I C K a sick person
D. a healthy person healthy H E A L T H Y a healthy person
E. heavy people heavy H E A V Y heavy people
F. thin people thin T H I N thin people
G. a strong person strong S T R O N G a strong person
H. a weak person weak W E A K a weak person

I. a good driver good G O O D a good driver
J. a bad driver bad B A D a bad driver
K. a sour fruit sour S O U R a sour fruit
L. a sweet fruit sweet S W E E T a sweet fruit
M. a nice dog nice N I C E a nice dog
N. a mean dog mean M E A N a mean dog
O. a light room light L I G H T a light room
P. a dark room dark D A R K a dark room

LESSON 3

PAGE 98 **3. B.** Read the sentences of 3. A. The students respond orally.

PAGE 100 **6. A.** Read the following passage. Tell the students that there are eighteen words missing, and instruct them to put a caret (ᴧ) wherever there is a word missing.

When my Aunt Ruth *was* young, she went around the world. *First,* she crossed the *Atlantic* Ocean to Europe, and then she went to Asia. Asia is the largest *continent,* and there was a lot to *see.* She saw the Gobi Desert and the highest *mountain* in the world, Mt. Everest. After Asia she went to *Africa* to see the longest river *in* the world, the Nile. Then she crossed *the* largest desert, the Sahara. Next, she went by airplane to the *coldest* continent in the *world,* Antarctica. From Antarctica, she went to Australia, the world's *smallest* continent. From Australia, she crossed the *largest* ocean in the world, the Pacific. It took her *six* months to go to all those places. When she got home, she said, "I *saw* the world's highest mountain, the *longest* river, the coldest continent, and the *hottest* desert. But now that I am home I *am* the happiest person in the world."

PAGE 100 **6. D.** Read the sentences of 6. C. The students write TRUE or FALSE on a sheet of paper.

Chapter 9

LESSON 1

PAGE 102 **1. A.** Read the following three times.

A. sofa
B. armchair
C. lamp

D. dresser
E. stove
F. oven

G. refrigerator
H. freezer
I. cabinets

J. dishes
K. pans
L. furniture

PAGE 103 **1. B.** Read the following. The students write the corresponding letters on the lines provided.

1. lamp
2. refrigerator
3. sofa

4. dresser and armchair
5. dishes and pans
6. furniture and oven

7. stove, freezer, and cabinets
8. sofa, armchair, and furniture
9. lamp, dresser, and dishes

10. pans, refrigerator, and freezer
11. stove, oven, and cabinets
12. refrigerator, stove, and furniture

1. C. Spell each word. The students write the words on the lines provided.

A. sofa S O F A sofa
B. armchair A R M C H A I R armchair
C. lamp L A M P lamp
D. dresser D R E S S E R dresser
E. stove S T O V E stove
F. oven O V E N oven

G. refrigerator R E F R I G E R A T O R refrigerator
H. freezer F R E E Z E R freezer
I. cabinets C A B I N E T S cabinets
J. dishes D I S H E S dishes
K. pans P A N S pans
L. furniture F U R N I T U R E furniture

PAGE 103 **2. A.** Read the following three times.

A. bedroom
B. bathroom
C. kitchen
D. living room
E. dining room
F. garage

PAGE 103 **2. B.** Read the following. The students write the corresponding letters on the lines provided.

1. dining room
2. bathroom
3. garage
4. bedroom and living room
5. kitchen and bathroom
6. living room and dining room
7. bedroom and garage
8. kitchen, dining room, and living room
9. garage, bathroom, and bedroom

PAGE 103 **2. C.** Spell each word. The students write the words on the lines provided.

A. bedroom B E D R O O M bedroom
B. bathroom B A T H R O O M bathroom
C. kitchen K I T C H E N kitchen

D. living room living L I V I N G room R O O M living room
E. dining room dining D I N I N G room R O O M dining room
F. garage G A R A G E garage

PAGE 104 **3. B.** Read the questions of 3. A. The students write YES or NO on a sheet of paper.

PAGE 105 **5. B.** Read the questions of 5. A. The students answer orally or in writing.

LESSON 2

PAGE 106 **1. A.** Read the following three times.

A. fire
B. hair dryer
C. mower
D. scale
E. hose
F. vacuum cleaner
G. rug
H. ladder
I. weigh
J. measure
K. light
L. move

PAGE 106 **1. B.** Read the following. The students write the corresponding letters on the lines provided.

1. ladder
2. hose
3. hair dryer
4. vacuum cleaner and mower
5. scale and fire
6. rug and vacuum cleaner
7. weigh, light, and measure
8. move, measure, and weigh
9. fire, light, and hose
10. move, rug, and ladder

PAGE 107 **1. C.** Spell each word. The students write the words on the lines provided.

A. fire F I R E fire
B. hair dryer hair H A I R dryer D R Y E R hair dryer
C. mower M O W E R mower
D. scale S C A L E scale
E. hose H O S E hose
F. vacuum cleaner vacuum V A C U U M cleaner C L E A N E R vacuum cleaner
G. rug R U G rug
H. ladder L A D D E R ladder
I. weigh W E I G H weigh
J. measure M E A S U R E measure
K. light L I G H T light
L. move M O V E move

PAGE 107 **2. B.** Read the questions of 2. A. The students answer orally or in writing.

PAGE 109 **4. B.** Read the questions of 4. A. The students answer orally or in writing.

LESSON 3

PAGE 110 **1. A.** Read the following two times. The second time, the students repeat each city name.

1. Vancouver
2. San Francisco
3. Los Angeles
4. Mexico City
5. Houston
6. Chicago
7. Montreal
8. New York
9. Atlanta
10. Miami

PAGE 113 **2. D.** Read the following questions. The students write "Yes, it was." or "No, it wasn't." on a sheet of paper.

1. Was it the waiter who taught the students how to serve food?
2. Was it the composer who taught the students how to write music?
3. Was it the computer science teacher who taught the students how to repair cars?
4. Was it the gardener who taught the students how to fly an airplane?
5. Was it the chef who taught the students how to cook food?
6. Was it the beautician who taught the students how to cut hair?
7. Was it the artist who taught the students how to grow flowers?
8. Was it the mechanic who taught the students how to repair cars?
9. Was it the pilot who taught the students how to fly an airplane?
10. Was it the English teacher who taught the students how to paint pictures?

PAGE 114 **3. A.** Read the following dialog. Tell the students that there are seventeen words missing, and instruct them to put a caret (∧) wherever a word is missing.

Tom: Did *your* sister like the lamp I *gave* her for her new apartment?
Lisa: Yes, she liked *it* a lot. She said it looked good with her *new* furniture.
Tom: Where *did* she put it?
Lisa: I think she put it in the living *room* behind her sofa. That was very nice of you to give *her* that lamp.
Tom: Well, I . . .
Lisa: You know, Tom, I *think* you like my sister.
Tom: Well, I . . .
Lisa: You are *always* asking about her.
Tom: Yes, well, I think she *is* really nice.
Lisa: That's what she *was* saying about you. She said, "Tom is really a *nice* person."
Tom: She did? Did she *say* that?
Lisa: I'm *going* to see her tonight. *Should* I say to her that you like her?
Tom: Well, I don't know *if* you should say that. But . . . you *can* say that I think she's really nice.

PAGE 114 **3. D.** Read the sentences of 3. C. The students write TRUE or FALSE on a sheet of paper.

Chapter 10

LESSON 1

PAGE 116 **1. A.** Read the following three times.

A. credit cards	D. rings	G. closet
B. wallet	E. bracelet	H. tool box
C. purse	F. necklace	I. jewelry box

PAGE 116 **1. B.** Read the following. The students write the corresponding letters on the lines provided.

1. closet	4. wallet and credit cards	7. tool box, jewelry box, and closet
2. rings	5. purse and jewelry box	8. necklace, bracelet, and rings
3. tool box	6. necklace and bracelet	9. wallet, credit cards, and purse

PAGE 116 **1. C.** Spell each word. The students write the words on the lines provided.

A. credit cards credit C R E D I T cards C A R D S credit cards
B. wallet W A L L E T wallet
C. purse P U R S E purse
D. rings R I N G S rings
E. bracelet B R A C E L E T bracelet
F. necklace N E C K L A C E necklace
G. closet C L O S E T closet
H. tool box tool T O O L box B O X tool box
I. jewelry box jewelry J E W E L R Y box B O X jewelry box

PAGE 117 **2. B.** Read the sentences of 2. A. The students write TRUE or FALSE on a sheet of paper.

PAGE 118 **3. B.** Read the questions of 3. A. The students answer orally or in writing.

LESSON 2

PAGE 121 **1. B.** Read the sentences of 1. A. The students write TRUE or FALSE on a sheet of paper.

PAGE 122 **3. A.** Read the following two times.

A. English–They speak English in the United Sates.
B. Spanish–They speak Spanish in Mexico.
C. Portuguese–They speak Portuguese in Brazil.
D. French–They speak French in France.
E. Arabic–They speak Arabic in Egypt.

F. Russian–They speak Russian in Russia.
G. Chinese–They speak Chinese in China.
H. Korean–They speak Korean in Korea.
I. Japanese–They speak Japanese in Japan.

PAGE 122 **3. B.** Read the following. The students write the corresponding letters on the lines provided.

1. English
2. Spanish
3. Chinese
4. French
5. Portuguese and Spanish
6. Korean and Japanese
7. Arabic and Russian
8. English, French, and Russian
9. Portuguese, Chinese, and Korean
10. Japanese, Arabic, and English

PAGE 124 **3. E.** Read the questions of 3. D. The students answer "Yes, they do." or "No, they don't." on a sheet of paper.

PAGE 124 **4. B.** Read the sentences of 4. A. The students answer orally or in writing.

PAGE 125 **5. B.** Read the sentences of 5. A. The students answer orally or in writing.

LESSON 3

PAGE 126 **1. A.** Read the following three times.

A. grapes
B. ketchup
C. lettuce
D. salad
E. beans
F. peppers
G. chili
H. toast
I. flour

PAGE 126 **1. B.** Read the following. The students write the corresponding letters on the lines provided.

1. lettuce
2. grapes
3. peppers
4. toast and flour
5. ketchup and salad
6. beans and chili
7. grapes, lettuce, and salad
8. flour, ketchup, and toast
9. beans, peppers, and chili

PAGE 126 **1. C.** Spell each word. The students write the words on the lines provided.

A. grapes G R A P E S grapes
B. ketchup K E T C H U P ketchup
C. lettuce L E T T U C E lettuce
D. salad S A L A D salad
E. beans B E A N S beans
F. peppers P E P P E R S peppers
G. chili C H I L I chili
H. toast T O A S T toast
I. flour F L O U R flour

PAGE 127 **2. B.** Read the questions of 2. A. The students answer orally or in writing.

PAGE 128 **3. A.** Read the following passage. Tell the students that there are eighteen words missing, and instruct them to put a caret (∧) wherever a word is missing.

My family and I *went* to a small town in Illinois where you *could* see how people lived in the 1800s. In those days, most *of* the people didn't *have* a lot of money. They couldn't buy things, *so* they made what they needed. My family and I saw how they *made* soap, and we *saw* how they made candles. We saw a man who was making horseshoes, and we saw women who *were* making clothes.

In those days, *people* got up at sunrise, and they worked all day. We saw the *kind* of food they ate. They didn't *eat* hamburgers, French fries, or pizza. They usually ate some kind of *meat* with potatoes and some kind of vegetable. They usually went to bed *before* 9:00 p.m.

Abraham Lincoln lived in *this* town. We saw the post office where he worked. He was a *young* man in those days. He liked to read. He read *every* book that he could borrow. The people in the town didn't *know* that he was *going* to be president of the United States.

PAGE 129 **3. D.** Read the sentences of 3. C. The students write TRUE or FALSE on a sheet of paper.

Chapter 11

LESSON 1

PAGE 130 **1. A.** Read the following three times.

A. a gallon of milk
B. a loaf of bread
C. a can of soup

D. a head of lettuce
E. a carton of eggs
F. a jar of jam

G. a bottle of soda
H. a bag of flour
I. a box of cereal

J. a pound of cheese
K. a bar of soap
L. a roll of paper towels

PAGE 131 **1. B.** Read the following. The students write the corresponding letters on the lines provided.

1. a carton of eggs
2. a bottle of soda
3. a gallon of milk
4. a bag of flour
5. a loaf of bread and a head of lettuce
6. a can of soup and a jar of jam
7. a box of cereal and a pound of cheese
8. a roll of paper towels and a bar of soap
9. a can of soup, a bottle of soda, and a box of cereal
10. a jar of jam, a bag of flour, and a roll of paper towels
11. a gallon of milk, a carton of eggs, and a pound of cheese
12. a head of lettuce, a loaf of bread, and a bar of soap

PAGE 131 **1. C.** Spell each word. The students write the words on the lines provided.

A. a gallon of milk gallon G A L L O N a gallon of milk
B. a loaf of bread loaf L O A F a loaf of bread
C. a can of soup can C A N a can of soup
D. a head of lettuce head H E A D a head of lettuce
E. a carton of eggs carton C A R T O N a carton of eggs
F. a jar of jam jar J A R a jar of jam

G. a bottle of soda bottle B O T T L E a bottle of soda
H. a bag of flour bag B A G a bag of flour
I. a box of cereal box B O X a box of cereal
J. a pound of cheese pound P O U N D a pound of cheese
K. a bar of soap bar B A R a bar of soap
L. a roll of paper towels roll R O L L a roll of paper towels

PAGE 131 **2. B.** Read the questions of 2. A. The students answer orally or in writing.

PAGE 132 **3. B.** Read the questions of 3. A. The students answer orally or in writing.

PAGE 133 **4. B.** Read the sentences of 4. A. The students write TRUE or FALSE on a sheet of paper.

LESSON 2

PAGE 134 **1. A.** Read the following three times.

A. She is going to brush her teeth, but she hasn't brushed them yet.
B. She is brushing her teeth.
C. She has brushed her teeth.
D. She is going to wash the car, but she hasn't washed it yet.
E. She is washing the car.
F. She has washed the car.
G. She is going to plant the flowers, but she hasn't planted them yet.
H. She is planting the flowers.
I. She has planted the flowers.
J. She is going to open the gift, but she hasn't opened it yet.
K. She is opening the gift.
L. She has opened the gift.

PAGE 134 **1. B.** Read the following. The students write the corresponding letters on the lines provided.

1. She is washing the car.
2. She is brushing her teeth.
3. She is going to open the gift, but she hasn't opened it yet.
4. She has brushed her teeth.
5. She is planting the flowers.
6. She has opened the gift.
7. She has planted the flowers.
8. She is going to brush her teeth, but she hasn't brushed them yet.
9. She is going to wash the car, but she hasn't washed it yet.
10. She is opening the gift.
11. She has washed the car.
12. She is going to plant the flowers, but she hasn't planted them yet.

PAGE 137 **4. B.** Read the questions of 4. A. The students answer orally or in writing.

PAGE 140 **3. A.** Read the following passage. Tell the students that there are eighteen words missing, and instruct them to put a caret (‸) wherever there is a word missing.

We know an old man who *has* a house in the mountains 100 miles *from* any city. He doesn't have electricity. He has *never* used a microwave, he has never used a *computer,* and he *doesn't* have any electrical tools. He cooks all his food over a *fire,* and he reads every book he *can* buy or borrow.

We went to visit *him* last summer because I wanted to *write* a story about him for our school newspaper. His house was *small* and clean, and he didn't have a lot of *furniture,* just a bed, a dresser, some chairs, and a table. He had a cow and *some* chickens and a vegetable garden.

He told *me* that he drove every month to a small town where there was a small library. I *could* see books on the chairs, books on the table, and books on the floor. There were books everywhere. Most of the books *were* library books, but some of them were books that he bought when he *went* to town. I asked him how many books he read each month and he smiled. He said that he didn't *know,* but he was reading all the books in the small town's library for the *second* time.

PAGE 141 **3. D.** Read the sentences of 3. C. The students write TRUE or FALSE on a sheet of paper.

Index